MAX LUCADO

LIFE LESSONS *from*

REVELATION

Final Curtain Call

PREPARED BY THE LIVINGSTONE CORPORATION

THOMAS NELSON
Since 1798

Published in Nashville, Tennessee, by Thomas Nelson. Thomas Nelson is a registered trademark of HarperCollins Christian Publishing, Inc.

Produced with the assistance of the Livingstone Corporation. Project staff include Jake Barton, Joel Bartlett, Andy Culbertson, Mary Horner Collins, and Will Reaves.

Editor: Neil Wilson

All Scripture quotations, unless otherwise indicated, are taken from The Holy Bible, New International Version®, NIV®. Copyright © 1973, 1978, 1984, 2011 by Biblica, Inc.™ Used by permission. All rights reserved worldwide. www.Zondervan.com. The "NIV" and "New International Version" are trademarks registered in the United States Patent and Trademark Office by Biblica, Inc. ®

Scripture quotations marked NCV are taken from the New Century Version®. Copyright © 2005 by Thomas Nelson. Used by permission. All rights reserved.

Scripture quotations marked NKJV are taken from the New King James Version®. Copyright © 1982 by Thomas Nelson. Used by permission. All rights reserved.

Material for the "Inspiration" sections taken from the following books:

And the Angels Were Silent. Copyright © 2004 by Max Lucado. Thomas Nelson, a registered trademark of HarperCollins Christian Publishing, Inc., Nashville, Tennessee.

The Applause of Heaven. Copyright © 1999 by Max Lucado. Thomas Nelson, a registered trademark of HarperCollins Christian Publishing, Inc., Nashville, Tennessee.

Glory Days. Copyright © 2018 by Max Lucado. Thomas Nelson, a registered trademark of HarperCollins Christian Publishing, Inc., Nashville, Tennessee.

In the Eye of the Storm. Copyright © 1991 by Max Lucado. Thomas Nelson, a registered trademark of HarperCollins Christian Publishing, Inc., Nashville, Tennessee.

Just Like Jesus. Copyright © 1998 by Max Lucado. Thomas Nelson, a registered trademark of HarperCollins Christian Publishing, Inc., Nashville, Tennessee.

A Love Worth Giving. Copyright © 2002 by Max Lucado. Thomas Nelson, a registered trademark of HarperCollins Christian Publishing, Inc., Nashville, Tennessee.

Max on Life. Copyright © 2010 by Max Lucado. Thomas Nelson, a registered trademark of HarperCollins Christian Publishing, Inc., Nashville, Tennessee.

More to Your Story. Copyright © 2011 by Max Lucado. Thomas Nelson, a registered trademark of HarperCollins Christian Publishing, Inc., Nashville, Tennessee.

Unshakable Hope. Copyright © 2018 by Max Lucado. Thomas Nelson, a registered trademark of HarperCollins Christian Publishing, Inc., Nashville, Tennessee.

When Christ Comes. © 1999 by Max Lucado. Thomas Nelson, a registered trademark of HarperCollins Christian Publishing, Inc., Nashville, Tennessee.

ISBN: 978-0-3100-8666-6

First Printing October 2018 / Printed in the United States of America

CONTENTS

HOW TO STUDY THE BIBLE

The Bible is a peculiar book. Words crafted in another language. Deeds done in a distant era. Events recorded in a far-off land. Counsel offered to a foreign people. It is a peculiar book.

It's surprising that anyone reads it. It's too old. Some of its writings date back 5,000 years. It's too bizarre. The book speaks of incredible floods, fires, earthquakes, and people with supernatural abilities. It's too radical. The Bible calls for undying devotion to a carpenter who called himself God's Son.

Logic says this book shouldn't survive. Too old, too bizarre, too radical.

The Bible has been banned, burned, scoffed, and ridiculed. Scholars have mocked it as foolish. Kings have branded it as illegal. A thousand times over the grave has been dug and the dirge has begun, but somehow the Bible never stays in the grave. Not only has it survived, but it has also thrived. It is the single most popular book in all of history. It has been the bestselling book in the world for years!

There is no way on earth to explain it. Which perhaps is the only explanation. For the Bible's durability is not found on *earth* but in *heaven*. The millions who have tested its claims and claimed its promises know there is but one answer: the Bible is God's book and God's voice.

As you read it, you would be wise to give some thought to two questions: *What is the purpose of the Bible?* and *How do I study the Bible?* Time spent reflecting on these two issues will greatly enhance your Bible study.

What is the purpose of the Bible?

Let the Bible itself answer that question: *"From infancy you have known the Holy Scriptures, which are able to make you wise for salvation through faith in Christ Jesus"* (2 Timothy 3:15).

The purpose of the Bible? Salvation. God's highest passion is to get his children home. His book, the Bible, describes his plan of salvation. The purpose of the Bible is to proclaim God's plan and passion to save his children.

This is the reason why this book has endured through the centuries. It dares to tackle the toughest questions about life: *Where do I go after I die? Is there a God? What do I do with my fears?* The Bible is the treasure map that leads to God's highest treasure—eternal life.

But how do you study the Bible? Countless copies of Scripture sit unread on bookshelves and nightstands simply because people don't know how to read it. What can you do to make the Bible real in your life?

The clearest answer is found in the words of Jesus: *"Ask and it will be given to you; seek and you will find; knock and the door will be opened to you"* (Matthew 7:7).

The first step in understanding the Bible is asking God to help you. You should read it prayerfully. If anyone understands God's Word, it is because of God and not the reader.

"The Advocate, the Holy Spirit, whom the Father will send in my name, will teach you all things and will remind you of everything I have said to you" (John 14:26).

Before reading the Bible, pray and invite God to speak to you. Don't go to Scripture looking for your idea, but go searching for his.

Not only should you read the Bible prayerfully, but you should also read it carefully. *"Seek and you will find"* is the pledge. The Bible is not a newspaper to be skimmed but rather a mine to be quarried. *"If you look for it as for silver and search for it as for hidden treasure, then you will understand the fear of the LORD and find the knowledge of God"* (Proverbs 2:4–5).

Any worthy find requires effort. The Bible is no exception. To understand the Bible, you don't have to be brilliant, but you must be willing to roll up your sleeves and search.

"Do your best to present yourself to God as one approved, a worker who does not need to be ashamed and who correctly handles the word of truth" (2 Timothy 2:15).

Here's a practical point. Study the Bible a bit at a time. Hunger is not satisfied by eating twenty-one meals in one sitting once a week. The body needs a steady diet to remain strong. So does the soul. When God sent food to his people in the wilderness, he didn't provide loaves already made. Instead, he sent them manna in the shape of *"thin flakes like frost on the ground"* (Exodus 16:14).

God gave manna in limited portions.

God sends spiritual food the same way. He opens the heavens with just enough nutrients for today's hunger. He provides *"a rule for this, a rule for that; a little here, a little there"* (Isaiah 28:10).

Don't be discouraged if your reading reaps a small harvest. Some days a lesser portion is all that is needed. What is important is to search every day for that day's message. A steady diet of God's Word over a lifetime builds a healthy soul and mind.

It's much like the little girl who returned from her first day at school feeling a bit dejected. Her mom asked, "Did you learn anything?"

"Apparently not enough," the girl responded. "I have to go back tomorrow, and the next day, and the next . . . "

Such is the case with learning. And such is the case with Bible study. Understanding comes little by little over a lifetime.

There is a third step in understanding the Bible. After the asking and seeking comes the knocking. After you ask and search, *"knock and the door will be opened to you"* (Matthew 7:7).

To knock is to stand at God's door. To make yourself available. To climb the steps, cross the porch, stand at the doorway, and volunteer. Knocking goes beyond the realm of thinking and into the realm of acting.

To knock is to ask, *What can I do? How can I obey? Where can I go?*

It's one thing to know what to do. It's another to do it. But for those who do it—those who choose to obey—a special reward awaits them.

"Whoever looks intently into the perfect law that gives freedom, and continues in it—not forgetting what they have heard, but doing it—they will be blessed in what they do" (James 1:25).

What a promise. Blessings come to those who do what they read in God's Word! It's the same with medicine. If you only read the label but ignore the pills, it won't help. It's the same with food. If you only read the recipe but never cook, you won't be fed. And it's the same with the Bible. If you only read the words but never obey, you'll never know the joy God has promised.

Ask. Search. Knock. Simple, isn't it? So why don't you give it a try? If you do, you'll see why the Bible is the most remarkable book in history.

INTRODUCTION TO
The Book of Revelation

An ancient legend tells of a general whose army was afraid to fight. The soldiers were frightened. The enemy was too strong. Their fortress was too high and weapons too mighty.

The king, however, was not afraid. He knew his men would win. How could he convince them?

He had an idea. He told his soldiers that he possessed a magical coin. A prophetic coin. A coin which would foretell the outcome of the battle. On one side was an eagle and on the other a bear. He would toss the coin. If it landed eagle-side up, they would win. If it landed with the bear up, they would lose.

The army was silent as the coin flipped in the air. Soldiers circled as it fell to the ground. They held their breath as they looked and shouted when they saw the eagle. The army would win.

Bolstered by the assurance of victory, the men marched against the castle and won.

It was only after the victory that the king showed the men the coin. The two sides were identical.

Though the story is fictional, the truth is reliable: assured victory empowers the army.

That may be the reason God gives us the book of Revelation. In it he assures victory. We, the soldiers, are privileged a glimpse into the final battlefield. All hell breaks loose as all heaven comes forth. The two collide in the ultimate battle of good and evil. Left standing amid the smoke and thunder is the Son of God. Jesus, born in a manger, is now triumphant over Satan.

Satan is defeated. Christ is triumphant. And we, the soldiers, are assured of victory. Let us march.

AUTHOR AND DATE

The author of Revelation identifies himself only as "John," and it is likely this was not a pseudonym but the name of a well-recognized person in the church. The historical evidence reveals the majority of early church fathers (including Justin Martyr, Irenaeus, Clement, and Origen) identified this individual as the disciple John, who along with Peter and James was a member of Jesus' "inner circle." Later church historians (including Eusebius and Jerome) believed the author was "John the Elder," an obscure figure mentioned only in fragments from Papias as residing in the city of Ephesus around the same time the work was believed to have been written. The author notes he is writing from the island of Patmos, a small volcanic isle off the coast of Asia Minor (see 1:9). Early tradition held the disciple John was exiled to this island at some point during the reign of the Roman emperor Domitian, which would place the writing c. AD 95. It is believed John was the last of Jesus' disciples to die, c. AD 98, at an old age.

SITUATION

Similar to the other epistles in the New Testament, the author of Revelation directs his work to a specific audience—in this case, church members in Ephesus, Smyrna, Pergamum, Thyatira, Sardis, Philadelphia, and Laodicea (all located in western Asia Minor)—who were facing some form of persecution for their belief in Christ and were tempted to revert to their former way of living. Unlike other New Testament literature, the author notes his work is also a book of prophecy (see 1:3; 22:7, 18–19), and as such is written in a style similar to the prophetic books of the Old Testament (especially Daniel and Ezekiel). Furthermore, the author employs a genre of writing that flourished c. 200 BC–AD 200 known as *apocalyptic* literature, which draws heavily on the use of symbolism and imagery (typically portrayed through a vision) to show how God would one day bring about the ultimate end of evil and establish a new heaven and a new earth for his followers. While the symbols John uses seem strange and even bizarre to us today, his readers would have understood he was encouraging them to stay true to Christ and persevere, for God knew the suffering they were enduring and would one day reward them for their faith.

KEY THEMES

- God has a plan and a future for the world.
- God will be ultimately victorious over evil.
- There will be a final accounting for our faith and our lives.
- There is a better world in store.

KEY VERSE

"He will wipe every tear from their eyes. There will be no more death" or mourning or crying or pain, for the old order of things has passed away (Revelation 21:4).

CONTENTS

LESSON ONE

A VISION OF CHRIST

*He laid His right hand on me, saying to
me, "Do not be afraid; I am the First and
the Last. I am He who lives, and was dead,
and behold, I am alive forevermore."*
REVELATION 1:17–18 NKJV

1

REFLECTION

Reunions with old friends and family members can stir up memories in us and also remind us of what that person was like. Think of a time when you saw a friend you hadn't seen in a while. How had that person changed? What new information did you discover from the encounter?

SITUATION

As the disciple John neared the end of his life, it is believed he served as an elder in the city of Ephesus until he was banished to the island of Patmos, located off the coast of Asia Minor, during the persecutions of the Emperor Domitian, c. AD 95–96. It was there, on that small rocky isle, that John states he heard the voice of Jesus as he was worshiping God. When John turned to look at Christ, he saw the glorified Lord standing among seven lampstands, which he would soon learn represent seven churches in Asia Minor. Jesus instructs John to write down a message to each of these churches and also record the vision that will be revealed to him.

OBSERVATION

Read Revelation 1:9–20 from the New International
Version or the New King James Version

NEW INTERNATIONAL VERSION

[9] I, John, your brother and companion in the suffering and kingdom and patient endurance that are ours in Jesus, was on the island of Patmos because of the word of God and the testimony of Jesus. [10] On the Lord's Day I was in the Spirit, and I heard behind me a loud voice like a trumpet, [11] which said: "Write on a scroll what you see and send it to the seven churches: to Ephesus, Smyrna, Pergamum, Thyatira, Sardis, Philadelphia and Laodicea."

[12] I turned around to see the voice that was speaking to me. And when I turned I saw seven golden lampstands, [13] and among the lampstands was someone like a son of man, dressed in a robe reaching down to his feet and with a golden sash around his chest. [14] The hair on his head was white like wool, as white as snow, and his eyes were like blazing fire. [15] His feet were like bronze glowing in a furnace, and his voice was like the sound of rushing waters. [16] In his right hand he held seven stars, and coming out of his mouth was a sharp, double-edged sword. His face was like the sun shining in all its brilliance.

[17] When I saw him, I fell at his feet as though dead. Then he placed his right hand on me and said: "Do not be afraid. I am the First and the Last. [18] I am the Living One; I was dead, and now look, I am alive for ever and ever! And I hold the keys of death and Hades.

[19] "Write, therefore, what you have seen, what is now and what will take place later. [20] The mystery of the seven stars that you saw in my right hand and of the seven golden lampstands is this: The seven stars are the angels of the seven churches, and the seven lampstands are the seven churches.

NEW KING JAMES VERSION

[9] I, John, both your brother and companion in the tribulation and kingdom and patience of Jesus Christ, was on the island that is called Patmos for the word of God and for the testimony of Jesus Christ. [10] I was in the Spirit on the Lord's Day, and I heard behind me a loud voice, as of a trumpet, [11] saying, "I am the Alpha and the Omega, the First and the Last," and, "What you see, write in a book and send it to the seven churches which are in Asia: to Ephesus, to Smyrna, to Pergamos, to Thyatira, to Sardis, to Philadelphia, and to Laodicea."

[12] Then I turned to see the voice that spoke with me. And having turned I saw seven golden lampstands, [13] and in the midst of the seven lampstands One like the Son of Man, clothed with a garment down to the feet and girded about the chest with a golden band. [14] His head and hair were white like wool, as white as snow, and His eyes like a flame of fire; [15] His feet were like fine brass, as if refined in a furnace, and His voice as the sound of many waters; [16] He had in His right hand seven stars, out of His mouth went a sharp two-edged sword, and His countenance was like the sun shining in its strength. [17] And when I saw Him, I fell at His feet as dead. But He laid His right hand on me, saying to me, "Do not be afraid; I am the First and the Last. [18] I am He who lives, and was dead, and behold, I am alive forevermore. Amen. And I have the keys of Hades and of Death. [19] Write the things which you have seen, and the things which are, and the things which will take place after this. [20] The mystery of the seven stars which you saw in My right hand, and the seven golden lampstands: The seven stars are the angels of the seven churches, and the seven lampstands which you saw are the seven churches.

EXPLORATION

1. How does John describe himself to his readers? What is his present situation?

_____

_____

_____

2. Why do you think the seven churches are symbolized as lampstands?

_____

_____

_____

3. What are some of the metaphors that John uses to describe Jesus' appearance?

_____

_____

_____

4. The image of the _sword_ (see verse 16) is a symbol of God's divine judgment. Why is it significant that John sees this sword coming from Jesus' mouth?

_____

_____

5. How do you think John felt to see Christ again? How did he react when he saw Jesus revealed this way in his vision?

_____

_____

_____

6. Why was John instructed to write down the things he saw?

_____

_____

_____

INSPIRATION

To envision John, we should imagine an old man with stooped shoulders and shuffling walk. The years have long past since he was a young disciple with Jesus in Galilee. Most of his friends are dead, and now, the Roman government has exiled him to the island of Patmos. Let's imagine him on the beach. He has come here to worship. The wind stirs the cattails and the waves slap the sand, and John sees nothing but water—an ocean that separates him from his home. But no amount of water could separate him from Christ. . . .

John is about to see Jesus. Of course, this isn't his first time to see his Savior. For three years he'd followed Christ. But this encounter was far different from any in Galilee. The image was so vivid, the impression so powerful, John was knocked out cold. "When I saw him, I fell at his feet as though dead" (Revelation 1:17). . . .

If you are puzzled by John's words, you aren't alone. The world of Revelation cannot be contained or explained; it can only be pondered. And John gives us a vision to ponder, a vision of Christ that comes at you from all angles. Swords and bronze feet and white hair and sunlight. What are we to make of such an image?

First of all, keep in mind that what John wrote is not what he saw. (Yes, you read that sentence correctly.) What John wrote is not what he saw. What he wrote is _like_ what he saw. But what he saw was so otherworldly that he had no words to describe it.

Consequently, he stumbled into the storage closet of metaphors and returned with an armload of word pictures. Did you notice how often John uses the word _like_? He describes hair like wool, eyes like fire, feet like bronze, a voice like the noise of flooding water, and then says Jesus looked like the sun shining at its brightest time.

The implication is clear. The human tongue is inadequate to describe Christ. So in a breathless effort to tell us what he saw, John gives us symbols. Symbols originally intended for and understood by members of seven churches in Asia. For us to comprehend the passage we must understand the symbols as the original readers understood them.

By the way, John's strategy is not strange. We do the same. If you open your newspaper to an editorial page and see a donkey talking to an elephant, you know the meaning. This isn't a cartoon about a zoo; it is a cartoon about politics. (On second thought, maybe it is a cartoon about a zoo!) But you know the symbolism behind the images. And in order for us to understand John's vision, we must do the same. And as we do, as we begin to interpret the pictures, we gain glimpses of what we will see when we see Christ.

Let's give it a go. (From *When Christ Comes* by Max Lucado.)

REACTION

7. How do you know that John had remained faithful to Christ throughout his life?

_____

_____

_____

_____

8. Why does John use imagery and symbols in describing the vision the Lord had given him?

_____

_____

_____

_____

9. What are some ways the media uses symbols today to communicate an idea?

10. In what way is John's depiction of Jesus different from the image of him in your mind?

11. How does John's vision of Jesus change the way you view Christ?

12. How can you help someone have a new awareness of Christ and his power?

LIFE LESSONS

God is never limited by our circumstances. In fact, he often uses them for his purposes. He knows that when we're isolated, we tend to be less distracted. So, just as he did with John, he will often put us in places where we will pay attention to his voice. We need to take our mental pictures of Jesus lightly but hold dear to the composite impression of his majesty, character, authority, and beauty. Like John, we don't worship idols or images, but Christ in the Spirit.

DEVOTION

Lord Jesus, you are more powerful than we could ever imagine. We stand in awe of your presence and fall at your feet in worship. To you be glory and authority forever and ever.

JOURNALING

How can this vision of Christ that John depicts be an encouragement to you if you are facing difficult times?

FOR FURTHER READING

To complete the book of Revelation during this twelve-part study, read Revelation 1:1–20. For more Bible passages on Christ's authority and power, read Matthew 28:18–20; Luke 4:33–36; 10:18–20; 1 Corinthians 15:22–24; 2 Corinthians 10:4–5; Ephesians 1:19–21; Colossians 2:9–12; and Hebrews 5:7–10.

LESSON TWO

YOUR FIRST LOVE

You have persevered and have endured hardships for my name, and have not grown weary. Yet I hold this against you: You have forsaken the love you had at first.

REVELATION 2:3–4

REFLECTION

Think about the first time you fell in love—the odd things it made you do and the (at least temporary) improvements it brought about in your life. What do you remember most about your first love? Why do these particular things stand out to you in your memory?

SITUATION

After Jesus appears to John in a vision and instructs him to "not be afraid" (1:17), he begins to dictate seven letters for John to write to seven churches in the region of western Asia Minor (modern-day Turkey). The sequence in which John writes these letters follows a rough geographic circle formed by the cities mentioned, beginning with the city of Ephesus, which was located on the western coast. Ephesus was a major trade center at the time and was also the center of worship for the fertility goddess Artemis (or Diana). While it is not known to what extent this contributed to the overall moral degradation of the population, it is clear from Jesus' words the believers there had been influenced by the culture and lost their *first love* for him.

OBSERVATION

Read Revelation 2:1–7 from the New International
Version or the New King James Version.

NEW INTERNATIONAL VERSION

[1] "To the angel of the church in Ephesus write:

These are the words of him who holds the seven stars in his right hand and walks among the seven golden lampstands. [2] I know your deeds, your hard work and your perseverance. I know that you cannot tolerate wicked people, that you have tested those who claim to be apostles but are not, and have found them false. [3] You have persevered and have endured hardships for my name, and have not grown weary.

[4] Yet I hold this against you: You have forsaken the love you had at first. [5] Consider how far you have fallen! Repent and do the things you did at first. If you do not repent, I will come to you and remove your lampstand from its place. [6] But you have this in your favor: You hate the practices of the Nicolaitans, which I also hate.

[7] Whoever has ears, let them hear what the Spirit says to the churches. To the one who is victorious, I will give the right to eat from the tree of life, which is in the paradise of God.

NEW KING JAMES VERSION

[1] "To the angel of the church of Ephesus write,

'These things says He who holds the seven stars in His right hand, who walks in the midst of the seven golden lampstands: [2] "I know your works, your labor, your patience, and that you cannot bear those who are evil. And you have tested those who say they are apostles and are not, and have found them liars; [3] and you have persevered and have patience, and have labored for My name's sake and have not become weary. [4] Nevertheless I have this against you, that you have left your first love. [5] Remember therefore from where you have fallen; repent and do the first works, or else I will come to you quickly and remove your lampstand from its place—unless you repent. ⁶ But this you have, that you hate the deeds of the Nicolaitans, which I also hate.

⁷ "He who has an ear, let him hear what the Spirit says to the churches. To him who overcomes I will give to eat from the tree of life, which is in the midst of the Paradise of God."'

EXPLORATION

1. For what specific things did Jesus commend the church in Ephesus?

_____

_____

_____

_____

_____

_____

_____

_____

2. How had the church in Ephesus dealt with false teachers in their community?

_____

_____

_____

_____

_____

_____

3. What in particular did Jesus say was lacking in the church?

_____

_____

_____

_____

_____

_____

4. In what ways could the Ephesians reconcile themselves to God?

5. What does it mean that the Ephesians' lampstand would be removed from its place if they didn't repent and turn back to Christ?

6. What does Jesus say he will do for those who are victorious in him?

INSPIRATION

I've always perceived John as a fellow who viewed life simply. "Right is right and wrong is wrong, and things aren't nearly as complicated as we make them out to be."

For example, defining Jesus would be a challenge to the best of writers, but John handles the task with casual analogy. The Messiah, in a word, was "the Word" (see John 1:1). A walking message. A love letter. Be he a fiery verb or a tender adjective, he was, quite simply, a word. And life? Well, life is divided into two sections, light and darkness (see 1 John

1:5–7). If you are in one, you are not in the other, and vice versa. Next question? . . .

But I like John most for the way he loved Jesus. His relationship with Jesus was, again, rather simple. To John, Jesus was a good friend with a good heart and a good idea. A once-upon-a-time storyteller with a somewhere-over-the-rainbow promise. . . .

Now what do you do with a friend? (Well, that's rather simple too.) You stick by him.

Maybe that is why John is the only one of the twelve who was at the cross. He came to say good-bye. By his own admission he hadn't quite put the pieces together yet. But that didn't really matter. As far as he was concerned, his closest friend was in trouble and he came to help.

"Can you take care of my mother?" Of course. That's what friends are for.

John teaches us that the strongest relationship with Christ may not necessarily be a complicated one. He teaches us that the greatest webs of loyalty are spun, not with airtight theologies or foolproof philosophies, but with friendships; stubborn, selfless, joyful friendships.

After witnessing this stubborn love, we are left with a burning desire to have one like it. We are left feeling that if we could have been in anyone's sandals that day, we would have been in young John's and would have been the one to offer a smile of loyalty to this dear Lord. (From *A Love Worth Giving* by Max Lucado.)

REACTION

7. Read John 19:25–27. How did John demonstrate that he would always stick by Jesus?

_____

_____

_____

_____

_____

8. In what ways, if any, has your love for God changed since you first became a Christian?

9. What are some ways you have found to reignite the flames of your love for Christ? What direction regarding this can you find in Jesus' message to the Ephesian believers?

10. Is it possible to keep your love for God intense and enthusiastic? Why or why not?

11. What are some practical ways to keep your relationship with God a top priority?

_____

_____

_____

_____

_____

12. In what ways can you motivate others to renew their relationship with Christ?

_____

_____

_____

_____

LIFE LESSONS

Most of us tend to drift from our "first love." We may still be busy doing the "works" that Jesus instructed us to do, but our hearts really aren't in the relationship. We're distracted. We've drifted. Acknowledging the loss is the first important step back toward love. The next step is to identify how our "works" have changed. Jesus complimented the present works of the Ephesians, but he also pointed out they had stopped their "first works." What did your original encounter with Jesus inspire you to do? How much of it have your *stopped* doing?

DEVOTION

Jesus, forgive us for getting distracted in our lives and for straying from you—our first love. Help us to renew our commitment to you. Bring us back into a right relationship with you. We pray that you will always receive glory and honor through the way we lead our lives.

JOURNALING

What would you say is primarily motivating your service and sacrifice for God?

FOR FURTHER READING

To complete the book of Revelation during this twelve-part study, read Revelation 2:1–7. For more Bible passages on putting God first, read Deuteronomy 5:7–10; 1 Samuel 14:36–38; Psalm 86:11; Matthew 6:33–34; Luke 10:38–42; 14:25–27; 1 Timothy 6:17–19; and 1 John 4:19.

NO COMPROMISE

Be faithful until death, and I will give you the crown of life. . . . He who overcomes shall not be hurt by the second death.
REVELATION 2:10–11 NKJV

REFLECTION

The desire for acceptance can be a powerful influence in our lives. It can cause us to alter our dress, language, and behavior in an attempt to be accepted by the group around us. Think of a time when you compromised in your life just to fit in. What was the result?

SITUATION

The next city Jesus addresses, Smyrna, was located forty miles north of Ephesus. Smyrna was a wealthy city and also a center of emperor worship, which often brought the Christians there into conflict with the Roman authorities. Jesus says he is aware of their difficulties—hardships that unfortunately are not yet over—and calls them to continued faithfulness. The next city Jesus address is Pergamum, located sixty-five miles north of Smyrna along the fertile valley of the Caicus River. Pergamum held the honor of being the Roman provincial capital and was an important religious center for a number of pagan cults. It appears the church included several groups whose teachings ran contrary to the true message of Christ. Jesus has strong words for them, calling them to turn back to him and promising a reward for those who are faithful.

OBSERVATION

Read Revelation 2:8–17 from the New International Version or the New King James Version.

NEW INTERNATIONAL VERSION

[8] "To the angel of the church in Smyrna write:

These are the words of him who is the First and the Last, who died and came to life again. [9] I know your afflictions and your poverty—yet you are rich! I know about the slander of those who say they are Jews and are not, but are a synagogue of Satan. [10] Do not be afraid of what you are about to suffer. I tell you, the devil will put some of you in prison to test you, and you will suffer persecution for ten days. Be faithful, even to the point of death, and I will give you life as your victor's crown.

[11] Whoever has ears, let them hear what the Spirit says to the churches. The one who is victorious will not be hurt at all by the second death.

[12] "To the angel of the church in Pergamum write:

These are the words of him who has the sharp, double-edged sword. [13] I know where you live—where Satan has his throne. Yet you remain true to my name. You did not renounce your faith in me, not even in the days of Antipas, my faithful witness, who was put to death in your city— where Satan lives.

[14] Nevertheless, I have a few things against you: There are some among you who hold to the teaching of Balaam, who taught Balak to entice the Israelites to sin so that they ate food sacrificed to idols and committed sexual immorality. [15] Likewise, you also have those who hold to the teaching of the Nicolaitans. [16] Repent therefore! Otherwise, I will soon come to you and will fight against them with the sword of my mouth.

¹⁷ Whoever has ears, let them hear what the Spirit says to the churches. To the one who is victorious, I will give some of the hidden manna. I will also give that person a white stone with a new name written on it, known only to the one who receives it.

NEW KING JAMES VERSION

⁸ "And to the angel of the church in Smyrna write,

'These things says the First and the Last, who was dead, and came to life: ⁹ "I know your works, tribulation, and poverty (but you are rich); and I know the blasphemy of those who say they are Jews and are not, but are a synagogue of Satan. ¹⁰ Do not fear any of those things which you are about to suffer. Indeed, the devil is about to throw some of you into prison, that you may be tested, and you will have tribulation ten days. Be faithful until death, and I will give you the crown of life.

¹¹ "He who has an ear, let him hear what the Spirit says to the churches. He who overcomes shall not be hurt by the second death."'

¹² "And to the angel of the church in Pergamos write,

'These things says He who has the sharp two-edged sword: ¹³ "I know your works, and where you dwell, where Satan's throne is. And you hold fast to My name, and did not deny My faith even in the days in which Antipas was My faithful martyr, who was killed among you, where Satan dwells. ¹⁴ But I have a few things against you, because you have there those who hold the doctrine of Balaam, who taught Balak to put a stumbling block before the children of Israel, to eat things sacrificed to idols, and to commit sexual immorality. ¹⁵ Thus you also have those who hold the doctrine of the Nicolaitans, which thing I hate. ¹⁶ Repent, or else I will come to you quickly and will fight against them with the sword of My mouth.

¹⁷ "He who has an ear, let him hear what the Spirit says to the churches. To him who overcomes I will give some of the hidden manna to eat. And I will give him a white stone, and on the stone a new name written which no one knows except him who receives it."'

EXPLORATION

1. What does Jesus say he knew about what the believers in Smyrna had endured?

2. Why did Jesus say the believers there did not need to fear what they were about to suffer?

3. How had the church in Pergamum demonstrated their faith?

4. What fault did Christ nevertheless find with the church in Pergamum?

5. Some of the believers in the church in Pergamum were eating food offered to idols. How was this a destructive compromise?

6. How do you strike the balance between being a part of your community enough to evangelize and keeping yourself separate from sinful practices?

_____

_____

_____

INSPIRATION

Heavenly rewards are not limited to a chosen few but are given "to all who have longed for [Jesus'] appearing" (2 Timothy 4:8). The three-letter word *all* is a gem. The winner's circle isn't reserved for a handful of the elite but is for a heaven full of God's children who "will receive the crown of life that the Lord has promised to those who love him" (James 1:12).

For all we don't know about the next life, this much is certain. The day Christ comes will be a day of reward. Those who went unknown on earth will be known in heaven. Those who never heard the cheers of people will hear the cheers of angels. Those who missed the blessing of a father will hear the blessing of their heavenly Father.

The small will be great. The forgotten will be remembered. The unnoticed will be crowned, and the faithful will be honored. "Be faithful until death, and I will give you the crown of life" (Revelation 2:10 NKJV).

Your day is coming. What the world has overlooked, your Father has remembered, and sooner than you can imagine, you will be blessed by him. Look at this promise from the pen of Paul: "At that time each will receive their praise from God" (1 Corinthians 4:5).

What an incredible sentence. God will praise each person who is faithful to him. Not the best of them, or a few of them, or the achievers among them, but *each one of them.*

You won't be left out. God will see to that. In fact, God himself will give the praise. When it comes to giving recognition, God does not delegate the job. Michael doesn't hand out the crowns. Gabriel doesn't speak on behalf of the throne. God himself does the honors. God himself will praise his children.

While we're not sure exactly what those rewards are, we do know they include heavenly applause, God's approval, and eternal life. What else would you want? (From *Max on Life* by Max Lucado.)

REACTION

7. What is the promise God gives to *all* who refuse to compromise their faith in him?

8. Why is it often tempting for people to compromise their values in order to "fit in" with the crowd? What does Jesus' message to the believers in Pergamum say about this?

9. What are some temptations you deal with on a regular basis that might cause you to compromise your faith? How do you tend to respond to those situations?

10. How do you know when you've done something that has "crossed the line" in terms of compromising your standards? What do you do to remedy those situations?

_____

_____

_____

11. In what ways can you have a relationship with someone of a different faith without compromising your own beliefs?

_____

_____

_____

12. What are some strategies you have seen the enemy use to convince believers in Christ to compromise their standards? Why do you think these strategies are so effective?

_____

_____

_____

LIFE LESSONS

Some compromises surprise us, while others lay siege to our souls. Sometimes we fold, while sometimes we hold—for a while. Some of us live under a cloud of remorse over past compromises we have made or fear about the future. But we need to allow that regret or fear to serve as a motivating for us to return to the Lord. We need to remember that as soon as we turn around and run to God, he meets us with open arms. He has given us his acceptance and adopted us into his own family. And unlike the accolades and praise of this world, which so quickly fades away, he has promised an *eternal* reward to *all* who remain faithful to him.

DEVOTION

Heavenly Father, we are so easily swayed by this world and its thinking. Forgive us when we compromise our faith in an attempt to fit in with those in the world and gain acceptance from them. Help us to stand firm as we face the many stumbling blocks ahead of us.

JOURNALING

What practices have you developed to keep you from compromising your faith and morals?

FOR FURTHER READING

To complete the book of Revelation during this twelve-part study, read Revelation 2:8–17. For more Bible passages on not compromising, read Exodus 8:25–29; Numbers 25:1–2; Joshua 24:14–15; 1 Kings 11:3–4; Ezra 4:1–3; 9:1–2; Daniel 1:1–23; and 2 Corinthians 6:14–18.

STANDING FOR THE TRUTH

To the one who is victorious and does my will to the end, I will give authority over the nations . . . just as I have received authority from my Father.

REVELATION 2:26–27

REFLECTION

In our fast-paced world today, we are bombarded with countless messages from advertisers, social media channels, and those who just want us to buy into their agenda. How are you affected by all these messages? How do you discern which are *true* and which are *false*?

SITUATION

The church in Thyatira, located approximately forty-five miles east of Pergamum, is the fourth city on the Lord's list. Although not a large city, it was important for its commerce in wool, linen, apparel, dyed materials, leatherwork, and bronze work. The city was home to an extensive trade guild, which appears to have played a prominent role in the lives of those in the city. Once again, Jesus' review of the believers there is mixed. While he commends them for their service and good works, he confronts them for being taken in by a charismatic figure who is spreading false teachings. Jesus appeals to his true followers to hold fast to what is right.

OBSERVATION

*Read Revelation 2:18–29 from the New International
Version or the New King James Version.*

NEW INTERNATIONAL VERSION

[18] "To the angel of the church in Thyatira write:

These are the words of the Son of God, whose eyes are like blazing fire and whose feet are like burnished bronze. [19] I know your deeds, your love and faith, your service and perseverance, and that you are now doing more than you did at first.

[20] Nevertheless, I have this against you: You tolerate that woman Jezebel, who calls herself a prophet. By her teaching she misleads my servants into sexual immorality and the eating of food sacrificed to idols. [21] I have given her time to repent of her immorality, but she is unwilling. [22] So I will cast her on a bed of suffering, and I will make those who commit adultery with her suffer intensely, unless they repent of her ways. [23] I will strike her children dead. Then all the churches will know that I am he who searches hearts and minds, and I will repay each of you according to your deeds.

[24] Now I say to the rest of you in Thyatira, to you who do not hold to her teaching and have not learned Satan's so-called deep secrets, 'I will not impose any other burden on you, [25] except to hold on to what you have until I come.'

[26] To the one who is victorious and does my will to the end, I will give authority over the nations— [27] that one 'will rule them with an iron scepter and will dash them to pieces like pottery'—just as I have received authority from my Father. [28] I will also give that one the morning star. [29] Whoever has ears, let them hear what the Spirit says to the churches.

NEW KING JAMES VERSION

[18] "And to the angel of the church in Thyatira write,

'These things says the Son of God, who has eyes like a flame of fire, and His feet like fine brass: [19] "I know your works, love, service, faith,

and your patience; and as for your works, the last are more than the first.
²⁰ Nevertheless I have a few things against you, because you allow that
woman Jezebel, who calls herself a prophetess, to teach and seduce My
servants to commit sexual immorality and eat things sacrificed to idols.
²¹ And I gave her time to repent of her sexual immorality, and she did not
repent. ²² Indeed I will cast her into a sickbed, and those who commit
adultery with her into great tribulation, unless they repent of their deeds.
²³ I will kill her children with death, and all the churches shall know that
I am He who searches the minds and hearts. And I will give to each one
of you according to your works.

²⁴ "Now to you I say, and to the rest in Thyatira, as many as do not
have this doctrine, who have not known the depths of Satan, as they
say, I will put on you no other burden. ²⁵ But hold fast what you have till
I come. ²⁶ And he who overcomes, and keeps My works until the end,
to him I will give power over the nations—

> ²⁷ 'He shall rule them with a rod of iron;
> They shall be dashed to pieces like the potter's vessels'—

as I also have received from My Father; ²⁸ and I will give him the
morning star.

²⁹ "He who has an ear, let him hear what the Spirit says to the
churches." '

EXPLORATION

1. For what does Jesus commend the believers in Thyatira?

_____

_____

_____

_____

_____

2. What does Jesus say that he holds against them?

3. How had "Jezebel" mislead some of the believers in the congregation?

4. Why do you think the believers were deceived by Jezebel's teaching?

5. What does Jesus say will happen to Jezebel as a result of her leading the believers astray?

6. What rewards does Jesus promise to those who stay true to him until the end?

INSPIRATION

Desire some glory days in your life? Engage with the Bible. Meditate on it day and night. Think and rethink about God's Word. Let it be your guide. Make it your go-to book for questions. Let it be the ultimate authority in your life.

Don't chart your course according to the opinions of people or suggestions of culture. If you do, you will make the mistake that one farmer's son made. The father sent the boy to prepare a field, reminding him to till straight lines. "Select an object on the far side of the field, and plow straight at it."

Later when the father checked on the boy's progress, there wasn't a straight furrow to be found. Every row was uneven and wavy.

"I thought I told you to select an object and plow toward it," the dad said.

"I did," the boy answered, "but the rabbit kept hopping."

A straight line, like a good life, requires an unmoving target. Set your sights on the unchanging principles of God. Let God's Word be the authoritative word in your world.

This decision rubs against the skin of our culture. We prefer the authority of the voting booth, the pollster, or whatever feels good.

Such resistance is not novel with us. When Paul wrote a letter to Timothy, the apostle was helping the young pastor deal with the rage of selfishness in the culture. Paul listed nineteen characteristics of the people (see 2 Timothy 3:1–5), each of which was a fruit of rebellion. The way to deal with such self-absorption? Return to the God's Word....

Are you clicking the "save button" on Scripture? We save truth when we deliberately and consciously allow what we've heard to become a part of who we are. Jesus said, "You will know the truth, and the truth will set you free" (John 8:32). As we know (save) truth, the truth makes us free from guilt, fear, anger. Saved truth has a shaping, reconfiguring impact on a heart. Only when you allow the truth of Scripture to be the authority in your life can you know that it works. (From *Glory Days* by Max Lucado.)

REACTION

7. Why is it so important for you to "think and rethink" on God's Word every day?

8. What is your typical practice when it comes to studying the Bible?

9. What truths from the Bible have you found to be especially helpful when you are faced with false teachings about Jesus or the church?

10. What are some of the ways God's truth has set you free from guilt, fear, and anger?

11. What attitudes or activities are you still tolerating that are not pleasing to God?

12. Read James 1:5. What promise does this verse contain for those seeking truth?

LIFE LESSONS

Much of Jesus' charge against the believers in Thyatira had to do with them minimizing the effects of sexual immorality. In modern times, the world has not ceased to downplay the devastation caused by sexual immorality. When the followers of Jesus begin to likewise shrug their shoulders and even condone this kind of behavior, the church loses its ability to speak to the world. We must be vigilant about our responses to the world's pressure to "lighten up" when it comes to caring deeply about the way we conduct our relationships.

DEVOTION

Jesus, help us to sharpen our listening skills to hear your true voice in the midst of the other voices in this world. Help us to turn to the Bible first for guidance and not the opinions or philosophies our culture promotes. Give us the strength to say no to the world and yes to you.

JOURNALING

What do you need to do to make reading and studying God's Word a priority this week?

FOR FURTHER READING

To complete the book of Revelation during this twelve-part study, read Revelation 2:18–29. For more Bible passages on spiritual discernment, read 1 Kings 3:10–15; Matthew 7:1–5; John 7:21–24; Ephesians 6:10–20; Philippians 1:9–11; Hebrews 5:12–14; James 1:5; and 1 John 4:1–3.

PERSEVERING FOR CHRIST

See, I have set before you an open door, and no one can shut it; for you have a little strength, have kept My word, and have not denied My name.
REVELATION 3:8 NKJV

REFLECTION

Everyone likes the *idea* of persevering, but it can be much more difficult to actually put it into *practice*—especially when faced with obstacles and setbacks. Think about a project you wanted to quit but ultimately chose to see to completion. What was the result of your perseverance?

SITUATION

Jesus' next message is for the believers in Sardis. This city, located thirty miles south of Thyatira, was once of great strategic importance to the Roman Empire. But by John's day its glory lay in the past, and its wealthy citizens had slipped into a form of moral "slumber" and decadence. Jesus says the church members are "are dead" (3:1), and he can only commend a few who have kept the faith. Christ then addresses the church in Philadelphia, located twenty-files miles southeast of Sardis, and issues a glowing report for the believers in that city. These followers of Christ had endured much for the gospel and had remained faithful to the Lord.

OBSERVATION

Read Revelation 3:1–13 from the New International
Version or New King James Version.

NEW INTERNATIONAL VERSION

[1] "To the angel of the church in Sardis write:

These are the words of him who holds the seven spirits of God and the seven stars. I know your deeds; you have a reputation of being alive, but you are dead. [2] Wake up! Strengthen what remains and is about to die, for I have found your deeds unfinished in the sight of my God. [3] Remember, therefore, what you have received and heard; hold it fast, and repent. But if you do not wake up, I will come like a thief, and you will not know at what time I will come to you.

[4] Yet you have a few people in Sardis who have not soiled their clothes. They will walk with me, dressed in white, for they are worthy. [5] The one who is victorious will, like them, be dressed in white. I will never blot out the name of that person from the book of life, but will acknowledge that name before my Father and his angels. [6] Whoever has ears, let them hear what the Spirit says to the churches.

[7] "To the angel of the church in Philadelphia write:

These are the words of him who is holy and true, who holds the key of David. What he opens no one can shut, and what he shuts no one can open. [8] I know your deeds. See, I have placed before you an open door that no one can shut. I know that you have little strength, yet you have kept my word and have not denied my name. [9] I will make those who are of the synagogue of Satan, who claim to be Jews though they are not, but are liars—I will make them come and fall down at your feet and acknowledge that I have loved you. [10] Since you have kept my command to endure patiently, I will also keep you from the hour of trial that is going to come on the whole world to test the inhabitants of the earth.

[11] I am coming soon. Hold on to what you have, so that no one will take your crown. [12] The one who is victorious I will make a pillar in the

temple of my God. Never again will they leave it. I will write on them the name of my God and the name of the city of my God, the new Jerusalem, which is coming down out of heaven from my God; and I will also write on them my new name. [13] Whoever has ears, let them hear what the Spirit says to the churches.

NEW KING JAMES VERSION

[1] "And to the angel of the church in Sardis write,

'These things says He who has the seven Spirits of God and the seven stars: "I know your works, that you have a name that you are alive, but you are dead. [2] Be watchful, and strengthen the things which remain, that are ready to die, for I have not found your works perfect before God. [3] Remember therefore how you have received and heard; hold fast and repent. Therefore if you will not watch, I will come upon you as a thief, and you will not know what hour I will come upon you. [4] You have a few names even in Sardis who have not defiled their garments; and they shall walk with Me in white, for they are worthy. [5] He who overcomes shall be clothed in white garments, and I will not blot out his name from the Book of Life; but I will confess his name before My Father and before His angels.

[6] "He who has an ear, let him hear what the Spirit says to the churches."'

'[7] "And to the angel of the church in Philadelphia write,

'These things says He who is holy, He who is true, "He who has the key of David, He who opens and no one shuts, and shuts and no one opens": [8] "I know your works. See, I have set before you an open door, and no one can shut it; for you have a little strength, have kept My word, and have not denied My name. [9] Indeed I will make those of the synagogue of Satan, who say they are Jews and are not, but lie—indeed I will make them come and worship before your feet, and to know that I have loved you. [10] Because you have kept My command to persevere, I also will keep you from the hour of trial which shall come upon the whole world, to test those who dwell on the earth. [11] Behold, I am coming quickly! Hold fast what you have, that no one may take your crown. [12] He who overcomes,

I will make him a pillar in the temple of My God, and he shall go out no more. I will write on him the name of My God and the name of the city of My God, the New Jerusalem, which comes down out of heaven from My God. And I will write on him My new name.

[13] "He who has an ear, let him hear what the Spirit says to the churches." '

EXPLORATION

1. What did Jesus say he knew about the believers in Sardis? How had they failed to persevere?

_____

_____

_____

_____

2. What did Jesus instruct the believers in that city to do?

_____

_____

_____

_____

3. How did Jesus describe himself to the believers in Philadelphia?

_____

_____

_____

4. For what in particular did Jesus commend the church?

_____

_____

_____

5. How did Jesus say he was protecting the church of Philadelphia?

_____

_____

_____

_____

6. Jesus promised rewards to the believers in that city for their continued perseverance and faith in him. What other promises did he make?

_____

_____

_____

INSPIRATION

"These are the words of him who is holy and true, who holds the key of David. What he opens no one can shut, and what he shuts no one can open. I know your deeds. See, I have placed before you an open door that no one can shut. I know that you have little strength, yet you have kept my word and have not denied my name" (Revelation 3:7–8).

Jesus is a doorman. He opens and shuts doors all the time, and no one can close what he has opened, and no one can open what he has closed. He stands at doors and knocks. "Here I am! I stand at the door and knock. If anyone hears my voice and opens the door, I will come in and eat with that person, and they with me" (3:20).

If the door is locked, he has a key. If he doesn't want to use the key, he walks through the walls (see John 20:19). But better than being just a doorman, Jesus _is_ the door. "I am the door. If anyone enters by Me, he will be saved, and will go in and out and find pasture" (John 10:9 NKJV).

So what is Jesus trying to say with all this talk about doors? He controls all gateways and passages from one place to another. Nothing gets past him without his knowing it.

Jesus doesn't leave us standing in the hallway or outside in the cold. He has something for us—new opportunities, new destinations, new chances to show our faith in him.

What do we do as we wait for other doors to open? In the book of Revelation, Jesus makes it clear to the church of Philadelphia—keep God's Word and commands, stay faithful, and don't curse or deny him.

Right now Jesus is sorting through that vast key ring, looking for the right door for you. He may have to lock and unlock a few other doors first, but one is sure to open soon.

Trust him. It's an open-and-shut case. (Adapted from *Max on Life* by Max Lucado.)

REACTION

7. What are some doors that you have seen Jesus open in your life?

8. When are some times you had to persevere as you waited for doors to open?

9. In what ways did you see God respond to your faithfulness?

10. Who has helped you persevere in your faithfulness? How did that person help you?

_____

_____

_____

_____

_____

11. In what ways has your church helped you stay faithful to God?

_____

_____

_____

_____

12. Think of someone you know who is struggling to stay faithful to God. How can you encourage him or her to persevere and not give up?

_____

_____

_____

_____

LIFE LESSONS

The challenge believers face each and every day is to stay true to Christ and practice faithfulness. To this end, the church in Philadelphia provides us with three crucial principles on how to stay faithful: (1) acknowledge our weakness and God's strength, (2) obey God's Word, and (3) claim the name of Christ. As we put these principles into practice, like our brothers and sisters from Philadelphia, we will also receive Christ's commendation.

DEVOTION

Father, help us to keep our eyes fixed on the promise and hope of heaven rather than on things of this world which so quickly pass. Guide us as we wait for your timing and lead us through the doors you want us to take. Help us to always stay focused on you when times grow difficult.

JOURNALING

What makes it the most difficult for you to persevere through trials?

FOR FURTHER READING

To complete the book of Revelation during this twelve-part study, read Revelation 3:1–13. For more Bible passages on perseverance, read Matthew 24:12–13; Mark 13:12–13; Romans 5:3–4; Galatians 6:7–10; 1 Thessalonians 1:2–7; 1 Timothy 6:11–12; Hebrews 12:1–3; and James 1:2–4.

LESSON SIX

VIBRANT FAITH

I know your deeds, that you are neither cold nor hot. I wish you were either one or the other! So, because you are lukewarm—neither hot nor cold—I am about to spit you out of my mouth.

REVELATION 3:15–16

REFLECTION

When your consider your faith in Christ, would you consider it to be more on the "hot" side (active and growing) side, the "cold" side (spiritually stuck), or more "lukewarm" (a mixture of both)? Where do you *want* your faith to be on the temperature scale?

_____

_____

_____

_____

_____

_____

_____

_____

_____

_____

SITUATION

Jesus' final message is to the believers in Laodicea. The residents of this wealthy city, located on a major trade route forty-five miles southeast of Philadelphia and one hundred miles east of Ephesus, specialized in the production of a glossy black wool. Hot and cold springs to the south of the city provided the citizens with a poor-quality and lukewarm water source. The inhabitants seemed to have learned the art of compromise and accommodation . . . and these traits were prevalent in the believers there as well. Unlike the other churches, Jesus had *nothing* good to say about their behavior—which was evidently as bland as the water that flowed into the city—saying only, "those whom I love I rebuke and discipline" (3:19).

OBSERVATION

*Read Revelation 3:14–22 from the New International
Version or the New King James Version.*

NEW INTERNATIONAL VERSION

[14] "To the angel of the church in Laodicea write:

These are the words of the Amen, the faithful and true witness, the ruler of God's creation. [15] I know your deeds, that you are neither cold nor hot. I wish you were either one or the other! [16] So, because you are lukewarm—neither hot nor cold—I am about to spit you out of my mouth. [17] You say, 'I am rich; I have acquired wealth and do not need a thing.' But you do not realize that you are wretched, pitiful, poor, blind and naked. [18] I counsel you to buy from me gold refined in the fire, so you can become rich; and white clothes to wear, so you can cover your shameful nakedness; and salve to put on your eyes, so you can see.

[19] Those whom I love I rebuke and discipline. So be earnest and repent. [20] Here I am! I stand at the door and knock. If anyone hears my voice and opens the door, I will come in and eat with that person, and they with me.

[21] To the one who is victorious, I will give the right to sit with me on my throne, just as I was victorious and sat down with my Father on his throne. [22] Whoever has ears, let them hear what the Spirit says to the churches."

NEW KING JAMES VERSION

[14] "And to the angel of the church of the Laodiceans write,

'These things says the Amen, the Faithful and True Witness, the Beginning of the creation of God: [15] "I know your works, that you are neither cold nor hot. I could wish you were cold or hot. [16] So then, because you are lukewarm, and neither hot nor cold, I will vomit you out of My mouth. [17] Because you say, 'I am rich, have become wealthy, and have need of nothing'—and do not know that you are wretched, miserable, poor, blind, and naked— [18] I counsel you to buy from Me gold refined in the fire, that you may be rich; and white garments, that you may be clothed, that the shame of your nakedness may not be revealed; and anoint your eyes with eye salve, that you may see. [19] As many as I love, I rebuke and chasten. Therefore be zealous and repent. [20] Behold, I stand at the door and knock. If anyone hears My voice and opens the door, I will come in to him and dine with him, and he with Me. [21] To him who overcomes I will grant to sit with Me on My throne, as I also overcame and sat down with My Father on His throne.

[22] "He who has an ear, let him hear what the Spirit says to the churches.""""

EXPLORATION

1. What was Jesus' primary complaint against the believers in Laodicea?

_____

_____

_____

_____

_____

_____

_____

2. What factors might have led to this complacency in the church?

_____

_____

_____

_____

_____

_____

3. Read James 1:6–8. What is the problem with being "lukewarm" in your faith?

4. The citizens of Laodicea were quite wealthy. Given this, why did Jesus call the church "wretched, pitiful, poor, blind and naked" (verse 17)?

5. What did Jesus say it would take for this church to get out of their miserable state?

6. What do you learn in this passage about who Jesus is and what he does?

_____

_____

_____

_____

_____

_____

INSPIRATION

Jesus and his disciples were walking to Jerusalem one Monday morning after spending the night in Bethany. He was hungry and saw a fig tree on the side of the road. As he approached the tree, he noticed that though it had leaves, it had no fruit. . . . It had the appearance of nutrition but offered nothing. It was all promise and no performance.

The symbolism was too precise for Jesus to ignore. So he does to the tree on Monday morning what he will do to the temple on Monday afternoon: he curses it (see Mark 11:11–14). Note, he's not angry at the tree. He's angry at what the tree represents. Jesus is disgusted by lukewarm, placid, vain believers who have pomp but no purpose. They have no fruit. This simple act slams the guillotine on the neck of empty religion.

Want a graphic example of this? Consider the Laodicean church. This church was wealthy and self-sufficient. But the church had a problem—hollow, fruitless faith. "I know your deeds," Jesus said to this group, "that you are neither cold nor hot. I wish you were either one or the other! So, because you are lukewarm—neither hot nor cold—I am about to spit you out of my mouth" (Revelation 3:15–16).

The literal translation is "to vomit." Why does the body vomit something? Why does it recoil violently at the presence of certain substances? Because they are incompatible with the body. Vomiting is the body's way of rejecting anything it cannot handle.

What's the point? God can't stomach lukewarm faith. He is angered by a religion that puts on a show but ignores the service. (From *And the Angels Were Silent* by Max Lucado.)

REACTION

7. Why is being lukewarm in your faith incompatible with being a follower of Christ?

8. What are some bold steps of faith that Jesus has called you to take in the past?

9. What characteristics might describe a "lukewarm" church today?

10. Why is it often easier for even believers in Christ to rely on themselves and their possessions instead of on God?

11. In what way is your current level of wealth affecting your spiritual devotion?

_____

_____

_____

_____

12. What are some areas in your relationship with God that are easy to neglect?

_____

_____

_____

_____

LIFE LESSONS

The age of tolerance and materialism in which we live might also be called the "lukewarm age." People are not expected to believe in anything firmly. It is so much safer to fill our lives with things and remain neutral, inoffensive, and . . . lukewarm. This cultural spirit can easily slip into our lives as believers in Christ. On a scale of 1 to 10, we may think our faith is a "safe 5." But Jesus' words to the church in Laodicea in this passage from Revelation make it clear of what he thinks of moderate faith. Our Lord would prefer _outright rejection_ to a so-so commitment.

DEVOTION

Father, it is easy for us to become complacent in our faith and lose the vibrancy we once had for you. Help us to never take our salvation for granted, and guide us as we make our decisions based on what important and eternal. Thank you for loving us and calling us back to you.

JOURNALING

What are some ways you can reignite your zeal for God and keep your faith vibrant?

FOR FURTHER READING

To complete the book of Revelation during this twelve-part study, read Revelation 3:14–4:11. For more Bible passages on hypocrisy, read Psalm 101:7; Matthew 6:5–7; 7:1–5; Luke 12:1–3; Romans 2:2–4; James 4:8; 1 Peter 2:1–3; and 1 John 4:20–21.

LESSON SEVEN

WORSHIPING GOD

*I heard the voice of many . . . saying with a
loud voice: "Worthy is the Lamb who was slain
to receive power and riches and wisdom, and
strength and honor and glory and blessing!"*
REVELATION 5:11–12 NKJV

REFLECTION

Think of a memorable worship experience you've enjoyed in your life. Was it something for which you prepared or an experience that caught you off guard? What aspects of it can you remember—the participants, setting, and activities? Why was this time so special to you?

SITUATION

John reports that after Jesus finishes relating the letters to the seven churches, he looks and sees a door standing open in heaven. He is immediately caught up "in the Spirit" (5:2), and there he sees a throne, a glorious One on the throne, and twenty-four elders bowing down and worshiping. The spotlight then shifts toward the great One on the throne and an ominous scroll he holds in his hand. One of the elders tells John that only the Lion of Judah is worthy to open the scroll, but when John looks out, he sees a Lamb looking as if had been slain. He realizes only Jesus—the Lion *and* the Lamb—is worthy to open the scroll and unfold the events to come.

OBSERVATION

Read Revelation 5:8–14 from the New International
Version or the New King James Version.

NEW INTERNATIONAL VERSION

[8] And when he had taken it, the four living creatures and the twenty-four elders fell down before the Lamb. Each one had a harp and they were holding golden bowls full of incense, which are the prayers of God's people. [9] And they sang a new song, saying:

> "You are worthy to take the scroll
>> and to open its seals,
> because you were slain,
>> and with your blood you purchased for God
>> persons from every tribe and language and people and
>>> nation.
> [10] You have made them to be a kingdom and priests to serve
>> our God,
>> and they will reign on the earth."

[11] Then I looked and heard the voice of many angels, numbering thousands upon thousands, and ten thousand times ten thousand. They encircled the throne and the living creatures and the elders. [12] In a loud voice they were saying:

> "Worthy is the Lamb, who was slain,
>> to receive power and wealth and wisdom and strength
>> and honor and glory and praise!"

[13] Then I heard every creature in heaven and on earth and under the earth and on the sea, and all that is in them, saying:

"To him who sits on the throne and to the Lamb
　　be praise and honor and glory and power,
for ever and ever!"

[14] The four living creatures said, "Amen," and the elders fell down
and worshiped.

NEW KING JAMES VERSION

[8] Now when He had taken the scroll, the four living creatures and the
twenty-four elders fell down before the Lamb, each having a harp,
and golden bowls full of incense, which are the prayers of the saints.
[9] And they sang a new song, saying:

"You are worthy to take the scroll,
And to open its seals;
For You were slain,
And have redeemed us to God by Your blood
Out of every tribe and tongue and people and nation,
[10] And have made us kings and priests to our God;
And we shall reign on the earth."

[11] Then I looked, and I heard the voice of many angels around the
throne, the living creatures, and the elders; and the number of them was
ten thousand times ten thousand, and thousands of thousands, [12] saying
with a loud voice:

"Worthy is the Lamb who was slain
To receive power and riches and wisdom,
And strength and honor and glory and blessing!"

[13] And every creature which is in heaven and on the earth and
under the earth and such as are in the sea, and all that are in them,
I heard saying:

> "Blessing and honor and glory and power
> Be to Him who sits on the throne,
> And to the Lamb, forever and ever!"

¹⁴ Then the four living creatures said, "Amen!" And the twenty-four elders fell down and worshiped Him who lives forever and ever.

EXPLORATION

1. Why were the hosts of heaven worshiping Christ in this passage?

_____

_____

_____

_____

2. Music was a part of this worship experience. How does music help you worship?

_____

_____

_____

_____

3. What attributes of God do you concentrate on in your worship?

_____

_____

_____

4. How do you see these attributes of God reflected in this passage?

_____

_____

_____

5. How would you feel if you were sharing in this worship service? Why?

_____

_____

_____

_____

6. What do you think it will be like to worship God in heaven this way?

_____

_____

_____

INSPIRATION

John and the other disciples would do it again. I'm confident they would. They would get into the same boat and ride through the same storm. They'd do it again in a heartbeat. Why?

Because through the storm they saw the Savior.

Read this verse: "Then those who were in the boat worshiped him, saying, 'Truly you are the Son of God'" (Matthew 14:33). After the storm, they worshiped him. They had never, as a group, done that before. . . . Only after the incident on the sea did they worship him. Why?

Simple. This time, they were the ones who were saved. This time, their necks were removed from the noose. Their bodies were plucked from the deep. One minute, they were dangling over the edge of the abyss, staring into the throat of the slack-jawed canyon. The next, they were bottom-plopped and wide-eyed on the deck of a still boat on a placid sea.

So they worshiped. They did the only thing that they could do when their death sentence was stayed at the eleventh hour: they looked to the Eternal Governor who gave the pardon and thanked him.

When you recognize God as Creator, you will admire him. When you recognize his wisdom, you will learn from him. When you discover his strength, you will rely on him. But only when he saves you will you worship him.

It's a "before and after" scenario. Before your rescue, you could easily keep God at a distance. Comfortably dismissed. Neatly shelved. Sure he was important, but so was your career. Your status. Your salary. He was high on your priority list, but he shared the spot with others.

Then came the storm . . . the rage . . . the fight . . . the ripped moorings . . . the starless night. Despair fell like a fog; your bearings were gone. In your heart, you knew there was no exit.

Turn to your career for help? Only if you want to hide from the storm . . . not escape it. Lean on your status for strength? A storm isn't impressed with your title. Rely on your salary for rescue? Many try . . . many fail.

Suddenly you are left with one option: God.

And when you ask . . . genuinely ask . . . he will come.

And from that moment on, he is not just a deity to admire, a teacher to observe, or a master to obey. He is the Savior. The Savior to be worshiped. (From *In the Eye of the Storm* by Max Lucado.)

REACTION

7. How did the disciples' view of Jesus change after the storm at sea?

_____

_____

_____

_____

8. What are some of the ways Jesus has delivered you through difficult times in your life?

_____

_____

_____

_____

9. How have these acts of mercy impacted your worship of Christ?

10. Why is worship important for you personally?

11. In what ways do you worship Christ in your church?

12. What style of worship do you enjoy the most? Why?

LIFE LESSONS

Worship on this side of eternity is like a "dress rehearsal" for worship in heaven. We are practicing at giving our attention to the One who is worthy—our wonderful Savior. This doesn't come easy to those who spend much of their time giving attention to things without eternal worth. The apostle John's vision reveals glimpses of heavenly worship that can inspire and guide our efforts to lavish praise and honor on our Creator, Redeemer, and Lord.

DEVOTION

God, we cannot thank you enough for your acts of mercy toward us. We lift our voices in praise to you, for you alone are worthy to receive honor, glory, and blessing. Thank you for continuing to guide us and deliver us. Holy, holy, holy are you, the Lord God Almighty!

JOURNALING

How can you incorporate more worship into your daily routine?

FOR FURTHER READING

To complete the book of Revelation during this twelve-part study, read Revelation 5:1–9:21. For more Bible passages on worshiping God, read 1 Chronicles 13:8; Psalms 81:1–4; 95:1–7; 100:1–5; Isaiah 12:4–6; Matthew 2:9–12; John 4:21–24.; and Colossians 3:14–17.

PATIENT ENDURANCE

This calls for patient endurance on the part of the people of God who keep his commands and remain faithful to Jesus.

REVELATION 14:12

REFLECTION

It's fun when our favorite sports team wins the game, but often we don't consider all the hard work and sacrifice they were willing to endure to secure that victory. When are some times in your life that you were willing to endure to succeed at a goal? How did that pay off for you?

SITUATION

John watches as Jesus opens the first seal on the scroll, which releases seven "seal judgments" (see 6:1–8:1) followed by seven "trumpet judgments" (see 8:2–11:19) against the earth. After the angel sounds the final trumpet, a dragon (representing Satan) appears, who wages war against a woman (Israel) and her offspring (see 12:1–17). John then sees two beasts rise from the sea, and they are given power to also wage war against God's people . . . and against the entire world (see 13:1–18). John's vision reveals that God will one day bring justice to the earth—and that those who patiently endure and remain faithful to Jesus will be rewarded.

OBSERVATION

Read Revelation 14:1–13 from the New International
Version or the New King James Version.

NEW INTERNATIONAL VERSION

[1] Then I looked, and there before me was the Lamb, standing on Mount Zion, and with him 144,000 who had his name and his Father's name written on their foreheads. [2] And I heard a sound from heaven like the roar of rushing waters and like a loud peal of thunder. The sound I heard was like that of harpists playing their harps. [3] And they sang a new song before the throne and before the four living creatures and the elders. No one could learn the song except the 144,000 who had been redeemed from the earth. [4] These are those who did not defile themselves with women, for they remained virgins. They follow the Lamb wherever he goes. They were purchased from among mankind and offered as firstfruits to God and the Lamb. [5] No lie was found in their mouths; they are blameless.

[6] Then I saw another angel flying in midair, and he had the eternal gospel to proclaim to those who live on the earth—to every nation, tribe, language and people. [7] He said in a loud voice, "Fear God and give him glory, because the hour of his judgment has come. Worship him who made the heavens, the earth, the sea and the springs of water."

[8] A second angel followed and said, "'Fallen! Fallen is Babylon the Great,' which made all the nations drink the maddening wine of her adulteries."

[9] A third angel followed them and said in a loud voice: "If anyone worships the beast and its image and receives its mark on their forehead or on their hand, [10] they, too, will drink the wine of God's fury, which has been poured full strength into the cup of his wrath. They will be tormented with burning sulfur in the presence of the holy angels and of the Lamb. [11] And the smoke of their torment will rise for ever and ever. There will be no rest day or night for those who worship the beast and its image, or for anyone who receives the mark of its name." [12] This calls for patient

endurance on the part of the people of God who keep his commands and remain faithful to Jesus.

¹³ Then I heard a voice from heaven say, "Write this: Blessed are the dead who die in the Lord from now on."

"Yes," says the Spirit, "they will rest from their labor, for their deeds will follow them."

New King James Version

¹ Then I looked, and behold, a Lamb standing on Mount Zion, and with Him one hundred and forty-four thousand, having His Father's name written on their foreheads. ² And I heard a voice from heaven, like the voice of many waters, and like the voice of loud thunder. And I heard the sound of harpists playing their harps. ³ They sang as it were a new song before the throne, before the four living creatures, and the elders; and no one could learn that song except the hundred and forty-four thousand who were redeemed from the earth. ⁴ These are the ones who were not defiled with women, for they are virgins. These are the ones who follow the Lamb wherever He goes. These were redeemed from among men, being firstfruits to God and to the Lamb. ⁵ And in their mouth was found no deceit, for they are without fault before the throne of God.

⁶ Then I saw another angel flying in the midst of heaven, having the everlasting gospel to preach to those who dwell on the earth—to every nation, tribe, tongue, and people— ⁷ saying with a loud voice, "Fear God and give glory to Him, for the hour of His judgment has come; and worship Him who made heaven and earth, the sea and springs of water."

⁸ And another angel followed, saying, "Babylon is fallen, is fallen, that great city, because she has made all nations drink of the wine of the wrath of her fornication."

⁹ Then a third angel followed them, saying with a loud voice, "If anyone worships the beast and his image, and receives his mark on his forehead or on his hand, ¹⁰ he himself shall also drink of the wine of the wrath of God, which is poured out full strength into the cup of His indignation. He shall be tormented with fire and brimstone in the presence

of the holy angels and in the presence of the Lamb. [11] And the smoke of their torment ascends forever and ever; and they have no rest day or night, who worship the beast and his image, and whoever receives the mark of his name."

[12] Here is the patience of the saints; here are those who keep the commandments of God and the faith of Jesus.

[13] Then I heard a voice from heaven saying to me, "Write: 'Blessed are the dead who die in the Lord from now on.' "

"Yes," says the Spirit, "that they may rest from their labors, and their works follow them."

EXPLORATION

1. John writes that the 144,000—those who are faithful to God—have the Lord's name written on their foreheads. How do you respond this idea that God has his "stamp" on *you*?

_____

_____

_____

_____

2. In what ways did the 144,000 demonstrate they had endured in their faith for Christ?

_____

_____

_____

_____

3. The 144,000 have God's "mark" on their forehead, which identifies they belong to him. What does this mean about those who have accepted the beast's "mark"?

_____

_____

_____

_____

_____

4. What do the angels in this passage say about those who do _not_ patiently endure for Christ?

_____

_____

_____

_____

5. What is the greatest struggle for you presently when it comes to following Christ?

_____

_____

_____

_____

6. What are some ways other believers—your "144,000"—have helped you to persevere?

_____

_____

_____

_____

INSPIRATION

"Let us run the race that is before us and never give up" (Hebrews 12:1 NCV). Had golf existed in the New Testament era, I'm sure the writers would have spoken of mulligans and foot wedges, but it didn't, so they wrote about running. The word *race* is from the Greek *agon*, from which we get the word *agony*. The Christian's race is not a jog but rather a demanding and grueling, sometimes agonizing race. It takes a massive effort to finish strong.

Likely you've noticed that many don't? Surely you've observed there are many on the side of the trail? They used to be running. There was a time when they kept the pace. But then weariness set in. They didn't think the run would be this tough. Or they were discouraged by a bump and daunted by a fellow runner. Whatever the reason, they don't run anymore. They may be Christians. They may come to church. They may put a buck in the plate and warm a pew, but their hearts aren't in the race. They retired before their time. Unless something changes, their best work will have been their first work, and they will finish with a whimper.

By contrast, Jesus' best work was his final work, and his strongest step was his last step. Our Master is the classic example of one who endured. The writer of Hebrews goes on to say that Jesus "held on while wicked people were doing evil things to him" (verse 3 NCV). The Bible says Jesus "held on," implying that Jesus could have "let go." The runner could have given up, sat down, gone home. He could have quit the race. But he didn't. "He held on while wicked people were doing evil things to him." . . .

Jesus lifted his eyes beyond the horizon and saw the table. He focused on the feast. And what he saw gave him strength to finish—and finish strong. Such a moment awaits us . . . we'll take our place at the table. In an hour that has no end, we will rest. Surrounded by saints and engulfed by Jesus himself, we will know the work is, indeed, finished. The final harvest will have been gathered, we will be seated, and Christ will christen the meal with these words: "Well done, good and faithful servant" (Matthew 25:23 NKJV).

And in that moment, the race will have been worth it. (From *Just Like Jesus* by Max Lucado.)

REACTION

7. How would you describe the "race" that believers in Christ run?

_____

_____

_____

_____

8. What is the promise for those who patiently "run the race" for Jesus?

_____

_____

_____

_____

9. How was Jesus able to patiently endure everything he faced and still do God's will?

_____

_____

_____

_____

10. How can you follow Christ's example when it comes to running your race?

_____

_____

_____

_____

11. What are some ways you can encourage those who have given up the race?

_____

_____

_____

_____

12. How does understanding Christ's ultimate victory help you persevere through setbacks?

_____

_____

_____

_____

LIFE LESSONS

None of us like the idea of suffering, whether that is due to a work situation, an illness, or crisis in our lives. But the reality is God *never* promised a pain-free life for his children. In fact, the pages of history are filled with the stories of true and faithful followers who endured all sorts of trials in the course of following God's call. What God does promise, as we see in passages like this in Revelation, is that our patience endurance will be worth it. There is going to be a time of judgment—in which God *will* all right the wrongs in our world—and we need to keep that in mind as we go about our lives. We want God's "stamp" on our lives so we will hear him say, "Well done, good and faithful servant!" (Matthew 25:23).

DEVOTION

Lord, thank you for promising to be with us every moment of our lives. May we persevere and patiently follow you wherever you lead. May our voices be lifted up as we thank you, worship you, and glorify your name forever.

JOURNALING

What are some areas in your life where you would benefit from more patience and endurance?

FOR FURTHER READING

To complete the book of Revelation during this twelve-part study, read Revelation 10:1–14:13. For more Bible passages on endurance, read Isaiah 40:28–31; John 16:31–33; Romans 5:3–4; 1 Corinthians 10:11–13; Colossians 1:9–12; 2 Thessalonians 3:4–5; James 1:12–15; and Hebrews 10:36–39; 12:1–3.

THE DEFEAT OF EVIL

Then the beast was captured, and with him the false prophet who worked signs in his presence. . . . These two were cast alive into the lake of fire burning with brimstone.
REVELATION 19:20 NKJV

REFLECTION

Have you ever competed in an event knowing that you were virtually guaranteed to win? How did that affect the way you saw your competitors? How did it affect your performance?

_____

_____

_____

_____

_____

_____

_____

_____

_____

_____

_____

_____

SITUATION

The final series of judgments that John witnesses are known as the seven "bowl judgments" (see Revelation 15:1–16:21), so called because they issue forth from "seven golden bowls filled with the wrath of God" (15:7). Many of these plagues mirror the ones inflicted on the Egyptians in the Old Testament: boils, blood, darkness, frogs, and hail (see Exodus 7:14–10:29). Following this, John is carried into the wilderness and shown a woman sitting on a scarlet beast (see 17:1–5). She is "drunk with the blood of God's holy people" (verse 6), and all in heaven rejoice when she is finally judged and brought down (see 18:20). John then hears a great roar in heaven as all shout praises to God (see 19:1–8). He looks and sees Jesus riding on a white horse, leading the great host of heaven. John stands in awe as he watches God's army crush the forces of evil.

OBSERVATION

Read Revelation 19:11–21 from the New International
Version or the New King James Version.

NEW INTERNATIONAL VERSION

[11] I saw heaven standing open and there before me was a white horse, whose rider is called Faithful and True. With justice he judges and wages war. [12] His eyes are like blazing fire, and on his head are many crowns. He has a name written on him that no one knows but he himself. [13] He is dressed in a robe dipped in blood, and his name is the Word of God. [14] The armies of heaven were following him, riding on white horses and dressed in fine linen, white and clean. [15] Coming out of his mouth is a sharp sword with which to strike down the nations. "He will rule them with an iron scepter." He treads the winepress of the fury of the wrath of God Almighty. [16] On his robe and on his thigh he has this name written:

KING OF KINGS AND LORD OF LORDS.

[17] And I saw an angel standing in the sun, who cried in a loud voice to all the birds flying in midair, "Come, gather together for the great supper of God, [18] so that you may eat the flesh of kings, generals, and the mighty, of horses and their riders, and the flesh of all people, free and slave, great and small."

[19] Then I saw the beast and the kings of the earth and their armies gathered together to wage war against the rider on the horse and his army. [20] But the beast was captured, and with it the false prophet who had performed the signs on its behalf. With these signs he had deluded those who had received the mark of the beast and worshiped its image. The two

of them were thrown alive into the fiery lake of burning sulfur. ²¹ The rest were killed with the sword coming out of the mouth of the rider on the horse, and all the birds gorged themselves on their flesh.

NEW KING JAMES VERSION

¹¹ Now I saw heaven opened, and behold, a white horse. And He who sat on him was called Faithful and True, and in righteousness He judges and makes war. ¹² His eyes were like a flame of fire, and on His head were many crowns. He had a name written that no one knew except Himself. ¹³ He was clothed with a robe dipped in blood, and His name is called The Word of God. ¹⁴ And the armies in heaven, clothed in fine linen, white and clean, followed Him on white horses. ¹⁵ Now out of His mouth goes a sharp sword, that with it He should strike the nations. And He Himself will rule them with a rod of iron. He Himself treads the wine-press of the fierceness and wrath of Almighty God. ¹⁶ And He has on His robe and on His thigh a name written:

KING OF KINGS AND LORD OF LORDS.

¹⁷ Then I saw an angel standing in the sun; and he cried with a loud voice, saying to all the birds that fly in the midst of heaven, "Come and gather together for the supper of the great God, ¹⁸ that you may eat the flesh of kings, the flesh of captains, the flesh of mighty men, the flesh of horses and of those who sit on them, and the flesh of all people, free and slave, both small and great."

¹⁹ And I saw the beast, the kings of the earth, and their armies, gathered together to make war against Him who sat on the horse and against His army. ²⁰ Then the beast was captured, and with him the false prophet who worked signs in his presence, by which he deceived those who received the mark of the beast and those who worshiped his image. These two were cast alive into the lake of fire burning with brimstone. ²¹ And the rest were killed with the sword which proceeded from the mouth of Him who sat on the horse. And all the birds were filled with their flesh.

EXPLORATION

1. Why do you think Christ is portrayed as a warrior dressed in a robe dipped in blood?

2. What is the significance of Jesus wearing "many crowns" (verse 12)?

3. How does this description of Jesus differ from your view of him?

4. Why do you think the armies of the beast believed they could defeat Christ?

5. Why didn't the armies fight even though they were ready for battle?

6. What does it mean for you that the beast has been defeated?

INSPIRATION

On several occasions I have known the name of the victor before the end of the contest. Being a pastor, I'm often unable to watch the Sunday football games. While I am preaching, the teams are playing. I don't complain, however, since I can always record the games. So I do.

Yet on many Sundays a well-wishing parishioner will receive a text or email and learn the outcome of the game and feel the burden to share it with me. I've considered wearing a sign that reads "Recording the game. Don't tell me anything!"

I remember one contest in particular. My beloved Dallas Cowboys were playing a must-win game. I'd been careful to set the recorder and was looking forward to an afternoon of first downs and touchdowns. I avoided any mention of the event. I even avoided eye contact with anyone I thought might spill the beans. I made it as far as my car in the parking lot when an enthusiastic fan shouted out to me, "Max, did you hear the news? The Cowboys won!!!"

Grrr. Gone was the suspense. Gone was the edge-of-the-seat anxiety. Gone was the nail biting and eye ducking. Yet even though I knew the outcome, I still wanted to watch the game. As I did, I made a delightful discovery. I could watch stress-free!

The Cowboys fell behind in the second quarter, but I didn't worry. I knew the outcome. We fumbled the ball with six minutes to play. I didn't panic. I knew the winner. We needed a touchdown in the final minute. No problem. The victory was certain.

So is yours. Between now and the final whistle, you will have reason to be anxious. You are going to fumble the ball. The devil will seem to gain the upper hand. Some demon will intercept your dreams and destiny. All that is good will appear to lose. But you do not need to worry. You and I know the final score.

The next time you smell his stinky breath, remind him of the promise he is loath to hear: "The God of peace will soon crush Satan under your feet" (Romans 16:20). (From *Unshakable Hope* by Max Lucado.)

REACTION

7. What should your attitude toward life be given that you know the "final score"—that Jesus will be victorious and triumphant over the enemy?

8. How should you live differently with this assurance that evil will ultimately be punished?

9. In what ways does this passage inspire you?

10. What evidence can people see in your life that you're part of Christ's victorious army?

11. What does it mean to you that Jesus is King of kings and Lord of lords?

12. In what way does this passage alter your view of the end times?

LIFE LESSONS

The importance of knowing that our side wins in the end becomes clear when we face defeats in skirmishes and ambushes. It helps us remember that victory comes from Christ and what he accomplished on the cross, not in our much smaller victories that Christ helps us achieve. But we can certainly *rejoice* over Christ's victory. The outcome has been decided. Satan, evil, and death have been defeated. The turning point in history was the cross. Everything else is "working out the details," and we get to enjoy the benefits of Christ's victory for eternity.

DEVOTION

Jesus, you are truly the King of kings and Lord of lords. We give you praise and glory, for you have defeated the evil one. Help us to remember we are assured of this victory and see ourselves as overcomers in Christ—not victims of the enemy. All victory belongs to you.

JOURNALING

How can you be a better soldier for Christ in the day-to-day battles you face?

FOR FURTHER READING

To complete the book of Revelation during this twelve-part study, read Revelation 14:14–19:21. For more Bible passages on the enemy's defeat, read Genesis 3:14–15; Isaiah 53:1–12; Daniel 7:11–14, 23–27; Ephesians 6:10–18; Colossians 1:13–14; Hebrews 2:14–15; James 4:7; and 1 John 3:7–10.

ALL THINGS MADE NEW

Then I saw "a new heaven and a new earth," for the first heaven and the first earth had passed away, and there was no longer any sea.

REFLECTION

Most of the major events in life include built-in anticipation. Waiting is part of births, growing up, graduations, weddings . . . very few things of importance come instantly! Think of a time when you anticipated an upcoming event. What was the waiting like? How did you handle it?

SITUATION

John watches as an angel descends from heaven, binds Satan, and the thousand-year reign of Christ begins on earth (see Revelation 20:1–3). Following this, Satan is "set free for a short time" (verse 3) and gathers an army for one last stand against God. But it is a futile attempt, for God quickly sends fire down from heaven to consume his forces. Satan is consigned to the lake of fire, from which he will never escape, and the final judgment of humankind takes place before the great white throne of God (see 20:4–15). It's then time for something completely *new*, as God reveals he has prepared a special place for those who belong to him. It's greater than anything we could ever imagine . . . and all God's children are welcome there.

OBSERVATION

*Read Revelation 21:1–8 from the New International
Version or the New King James Version.*

NEW INTERNATIONAL VERSION

[1] Then I saw "a new heaven and a new earth," for the first heaven and the first earth had passed away, and there was no longer any sea. [2] I saw the Holy City, the new Jerusalem, coming down out of heaven from God, prepared as a bride beautifully dressed for her husband. [3] And I heard a loud voice from the throne saying, "Look! God's dwelling place is now among the people, and he will dwell with them. They will be his people, and God himself will be with them and be their God. [4] 'He will wipe every tear from their eyes. There will be no more death' or mourning or crying or pain, for the old order of things has passed away."

[5] He who was seated on the throne said, "I am making everything new!" Then he said, "Write this down, for these words are trustworthy and true."

[6] He said to me: "It is done. I am the Alpha and the Omega, the Beginning and the End. To the thirsty I will give water without cost from the spring of the water of life. [7] Those who are victorious will inherit all this, and I will be their God and they will be my children. [8] But the cowardly, the unbelieving, the vile, the murderers, the sexually immoral, those who practice magic arts, the idolaters and all liars—they will be consigned to the fiery lake of burning sulfur. This is the second death."

NEW KING JAMES VERSION

[1] Now I saw a new heaven and a new earth, for the first heaven and the first earth had passed away. Also there was no more sea. [2] Then I, John, saw the holy city, New Jerusalem, coming down out of heaven from God, prepared as a bride adorned for her husband. [3] And I heard a loud voice from heaven saying, "Behold, the tabernacle of God is with men, and He will dwell with them, and they shall be His people. God Himself will be

with them and be their God. [4] And God will wipe away every tear from their eyes; there shall be no more death, nor sorrow, nor crying. There shall be no more pain, for the former things have passed away."

[5] Then He who sat on the throne said, "Behold, I make all things new." And He said to me, "Write, for these words are true and faithful."

[6] And He said to me, "It is done! I am the Alpha and the Omega, the Beginning and the End. I will give of the fountain of the water of life freely to him who thirsts. [7] He who overcomes shall inherit all things, and I will be his God and he shall be My son. [8] But the cowardly, unbelieving, abominable, murderers, sexually immoral, sorcerers, idolaters, and all liars shall have their part in the lake which burns with fire and brimstone, which is the second death."

EXPLORATION

1. What is significant about the new city being described as a bride?

2. What does the voice from heaven say about this new city?

3. What will notably be *absent* in this new city?

4. How would you describe the future citizens of the new city?

5. In what ways will our relationship with God be different in the new city?

6. Why will some people not be a part of the new city?

INSPIRATION

The most hopeful words of this passage from Revelation are those of God's resolve: "I am making everything new!" (Revelation 21:5).

It's hard to see things grow old. The town in which I grew up is growing old. I was there some time ago. Some of the buildings are boarded up. Some of the houses are torn down. Some of my teachers are retired; some are buried. The old movie house where I took my dates has a "For Sale" on the marquee, long since outdated by the newer theaters that give you eight choices. The only visitors to the drive-in theater are tumbleweeds and rodents. Memories of first dates and senior proms are weather-worn by the endless rain of years. High school sweethearts are divorced. A cheerleader died of an aneurysm. Our fastest halfback is buried only a few plots from my own father.

I wish I could make it all new again. I wish I could blow the dust off the streets. I wish I could walk through the familiar neighborhood, and wave at the familiar faces, and pet the familiar dogs, and hit one more home run in the Little League park. I wish I could walk down Main Street and call out to the merchants that have retired and open the doors that have been boarded up. I wish I could make everything new . . . but I can't . . .

I can't. But God can. "He restores my soul," wrote the shepherd (Psalm 23:3 NKJV). He doesn't reform; he restores. He doesn't camouflage the old; he restores the new. The Master Builder will pull out the original plan and restore it. He will restore the vigor. He will restore the energy. He will restore the hope. He will restore the soul.

When you see how this world grows stooped and weary and then read of a home where everything is made new . . . tell me, doesn't that make you want to go home?

What would you give in exchange for a home like that? Would you really rather have a few possessions on earth than eternal possessions in heaven? Would you really choose a life of slavery to passion over a life of freedom? Would you honestly give up all of your heavenly mansions for a second-rate sleazy motel on earth?

"Rejoice and be glad," Jesus said, "because great is your reward in heaven" (Matthew 5:12). He must have smiled when he said that line. His eyes must have danced, and his hand must have pointed skyward. For he should know. It was his idea. It was his home. (From *The Applause of Heaven* by Max Lucado.)

REACTION

7. What are some of the things you've been sad to see grow old on this earth?

_____

_____

_____

_____

_____

8. What are you most looking forward to seeing or experiencing in the heaven and earth?

_____

_____

_____

_____

_____

9. What are some words that describe what you think it will be like to spend eternity with God?

_____

_____

_____

_____

10. What tends to cause you to take your eyes off your wonderful future with God?

11. Why do you think people still choose to give up their "heavenly mansions for a second-rate sleazy motel on earth"?

12. What are some of your responsibilities until the new heaven and new earth come?

LIFE LESSONS

We have a difficult time thinking about heaven without unconsciously smuggling earthbound thinking into it. All the elements of this life that make us tired, confused, bored, stressed, and overwhelmed will be gone. Yet just because we can't easily imagine ourselves in a heavenly setting doesn't mean God can't change us to fit it perfectly! We can trust that he will take care of the details in ways that will surprise and delight us. We can give our full attention to opportunities God places in our lives to pass on the good news to others, in the hope that they, too, will be citizens of God's eternal kingdom.

DEVOTION

Father, we look forward to that new city where we will eternally dwell with you. We hold to the promise that there will be no more sorrow or pain and that all things will be made new. Keep our eyes focused on these things . . . so we can remain faithful to you.

JOURNALING

How can you prepare *now* for the new heaven and new earth *to come*?

FOR FURTHER READING

To complete the book of Revelation during this twelve-part study, read Revelation 20:1–21:8. For more Bible passages on God's restoration, read Psalm 51:12; Isaiah 61:7; Jeremiah 29:10–14; 30:12–17; Joel 2:25–26; Zechariah 9:12; John 3:16; Acts 3:19–21; 2 Corinthians 5:16–17; Hebrews 12:22–24; and 2 Peter 3:10–13.

AN ETERNAL DWELLING

The city had no need of the sun or of the moon to shine in it, for the glory of God illuminated it. . . . And the nations of those who are saved shall walk in its light, and the kings of the earth bring their glory and honor into it.

REVELATION 21:23–24 NKJV

REFLECTION

Think about two cities in which you would enjoy living—including one or two positive and negative features about each one. Now, try to imagine a city with no evil whatsoever. How would you describe it? What makes it different even from the desirable cities you mentioned?

SITUATION

John is amazed as he witnesses the Holy City, the New Jerusalem, coming down out of heaven and descending to the earth. He hears a voice telling him that God will now *forever* dwell among his people, and there will be no more death, or mourning, or crying, or pain. An angel then takes John to the top of a mountain, where he is able to witness the full brilliance of the city for himself. John notices there is no temple in the city, for the "Lord God Almighty and the Lamb are its temple" (Revelation 21:22). John's vision stretches our imagination to the limits . . . and fills those of us who expect to live there one day with hope and great comfort.

OBSERVATION

*Read Revelation 21:9–27 from the New International
Version or the New King James Version.*

NEW INTERNATIONAL VERSION

[9] One of the seven angels who had the seven bowls full of the seven last plagues came and said to me, "Come, I will show you the bride, the wife of the Lamb." [10] And he carried me away in the Spirit to a mountain great and high, and showed me the Holy City, Jerusalem, coming down out of heaven from God. [11] It shone with the glory of God, and its brilliance was like that of a very precious jewel, like a jasper, clear as crystal. [12] It had a great, high wall with twelve gates, and with twelve angels at the gates. On the gates were written the names of the twelve tribes of Israel. [13] There were three gates on the east, three on the north, three on the south and three on the west. [14] The wall of the city had twelve foundations, and on them were the names of the twelve apostles of the Lamb.

[15] The angel who talked with me had a measuring rod of gold to measure the city, its gates and its walls. [16] The city was laid out like a square, as long as it was wide. He measured the city with the rod and found it to be 12,000 stadia in length, and as wide and high as it is long. [17] The angel measured the wall using human measurement, and it was 144 cubits thick. [18] The wall was made of jasper, and the city of pure gold, as pure as glass. [19] The foundations of the city walls were decorated with every kind of precious stone. The first foundation was jasper, the second sapphire, the third agate, the fourth emerald, [20] the fifth onyx, the sixth ruby, the seventh chrysolite, the eighth beryl, the ninth topaz, the tenth turquoise, the eleventh jacinth, and the twelfth amethyst. [21] The twelve gates were twelve pearls, each gate made of a single pearl. The great street of the city was of gold, as pure as transparent glass.

[22] I did not see a temple in the city, because the Lord God Almighty and the Lamb are its temple. [23] The city does not need the sun or the moon to shine on it, for the glory of God gives it light, and the Lamb is

its lamp. ²⁴ The nations will walk by its light, and the kings of the earth will bring their splendor into it. ²⁵ On no day will its gates ever be shut, for there will be no night there. ²⁶ The glory and honor of the nations will be brought into it. ²⁷ Nothing impure will ever enter it, nor will anyone who does what is shameful or deceitful, but only those whose names are written in the Lamb's book of life.

NEW KING JAMES VERSION

⁹ Then one of the seven angels who had the seven bowls filled with the seven last plagues came to me and talked with me, saying, "Come, I will show you the bride, the Lamb's wife." ¹⁰ And he carried me away in the Spirit to a great and high mountain, and showed me the great city, the holy Jerusalem, descending out of heaven from God, ¹¹ having the glory of God. Her light was like a most precious stone, like a jasper stone, clear as crystal. ¹² Also she had a great and high wall with twelve gates, and twelve angels at the gates, and names written on them, which are the names of the twelve tribes of the children of Israel: ¹³ three gates on the east, three gates on the north, three gates on the south, and three gates on the west.

¹⁴ Now the wall of the city had twelve foundations, and on them were the names of the twelve apostles of the Lamb. ¹⁵ And he who talked with me had a gold reed to measure the city, its gates, and its wall. ¹⁶ The city is laid out as a square; its length is as great as its breadth. And he measured the city with the reed: twelve thousand furlongs. Its length, breadth, and height are equal. ¹⁷ Then he measured its wall: one hundred and forty-four cubits, according to the measure of a man, that is, of an angel. ¹⁸ The construction of its wall was of jasper; and the city was pure gold, like clear glass. ¹⁹ The foundations of the wall of the city were adorned with all kinds of precious stones: the first foundation was jasper, the second sapphire, the third chalcedony, the fourth emerald, ²⁰ the fifth sardonyx, the sixth sardius, the seventh chrysolite, the eighth beryl, the ninth topaz, the tenth chrysoprase, the eleventh jacinth, and the twelfth amethyst. ²¹ The twelve gates were twelve pearls: each individual gate was of one pearl. And the street of the city was pure gold, like transparent glass.

[22] But I saw no temple in it, for the Lord God Almighty and the Lamb are its temple. [23] The city had no need of the sun or of the moon to shine in it, for the glory of God illuminated it. The Lamb is its light. [24] And the nations of those who are saved shall walk in its light, and the kings of the earth bring their glory and honor into it. [25] Its gates shall not be shut at all by day (there shall be no night there). [26] And they shall bring the glory and the honor of the nations into it. [27] But there shall by no means enter it anything that defiles, or causes an abomination or a lie, but only those who are written in the Lamb's Book of Life.

EXPLORATION

1. What is unique about the walls and gates of the New Jerusalem?

2. What is significant about the fact that the names of the twelve apostles (disciples) are written on the foundations of the city?

3. Why is there be no need for a temple in the New Jerusalem?

4. What parts of the spectacular description of the city are most meaningful to you? Why?

5. How can a person's place in the city be secured?

6. What does this passage reveal about God's ultimate plan?

INSPIRATION

One time, I took my nephew and niece to the San Antonio Zoo, a perfect place for a three- and a five-year-old to spend a Saturday afternoon.

A veteran kid-guide, I knew the path to take. Start small and end wild. We began with the lowly, glass-caged reptiles. Next we oohed and aahed at the parrots and pink flamingos. We fed the sheep in the petting zoo and tossed crumbs to the fish in the pond. But all along I kept telling Lawson and Callie, "We're getting closer to the big animals. Elephants and tigers are just around the corner."

Finally we reached the Africa section. For full effect I told them to enter with their heads down and their eyes on the sidewalk. I walked them right up to the elephant fence.

And just when I was about to tell them to lift their eyes, Lawson made a discovery. "Look, a doodlebug!"

"Where?" Callie asked.

"Here!" He squatted down and placed the pellet-sized insect in the palm of his hand and began to roll it around.

"Let me see it!" Callie said.

I couldn't lure them away. "Hey, guys, this is the jungle section."

No response.

"Don't you want to see the wild animals?"

No, they focused on the bug. There we stood, elephants to our left, lions to our right, only a stone's throw from hippos and leopards, and what were they doing? Playing with a doodlebug.

Don't we all? Myriads of mighty angels encircle us, the presence of our Maker engulfs us, the witness of a thousand galaxies and constellations calls to us, the flowing tide of God's history carries us, the crowning of Christ as King of the universe awaits us, but we can't get our eyes off the doodlebugs of life: paychecks, gadgets, vacations, and weekends.

Open your eyes, Christ invites. Lift up your gaze. "Seek first the kingdom of God" (Matthew 6:33 NKJV). Limit your world to the doodlebugs of this life, and, mark it down, you will be disappointed. Limit your story to the days between your birth and death, and brace yourself for a sad ending.

You were made for more than this life. (From *More to Your Story* by Max Lucado.)

REACTION

7. Why is it so easy to get focused on the "doodlebugs" of life and miss the spectacular wonders of God that are all around us?

8. In what ways are you anticipating your new home?

9. What are you doing to prepare for your future in the new city?

10. Knowing that your future dwelling is this heavenly city, how has your perspective of your earthly home changed?

11. In what ways does the image of this future home that John depicts in the book of Revelation help you deal to with death?

_____

_____

_____

12. How can this passage help you to encourage someone who has lost important earthly possessions?

_____

_____

_____

LIFE LESSONS

When we really see for ourselves the things that John saw, our "life lessons" will be over, replaced with the glories of our eternal home. The word *home* includes both the idea of place and of relationship. This is especially true of the New Jerusalem. It is a place we will live in a relationship with God. Yet there's no temple. No "place" is needed to meet God—because God's glory is everywhere! We are growing in our desire for our eternal home when we are less concerned with what we will do there than with *who* is there. What joy there will be in the Lord's presence and in the grand company of others when that moment comes.

DEVOTION

God of heaven, we see your hand stretching out as far as the east is from the west. We see your plan at work in our lives and how you are moving in our world today. Put your arms around us and embrace us. Take us home. May we be yours forever.

JOURNALING

How does the realization that you have an eternal dwelling with God give you peace in your life?

FOR FURTHER READING

To complete the book of Revelation during this twelve-part study, read Revelation 21:9–27. For more Bible passages on eternal life, read Matthew 25:41–46; Luke 23:39–43; John 17:1–3; Romans 6:23; 10:13; 1 Corinthians 2:9–10; 1 Timothy 6:17–19; Hebrews 12:22–24; and 2 Peter 3:13.

JESUS IS RETURNING

"Look, I am coming soon! My reward is with me, and I will give to each person according to what they have done."
REVELATION 22:12

REFLECTION

It's probably anyone's guess which experience is harder: waiting to arrive at a destination or waiting for someone special to arrive. Think of a time when you were waiting for someone to return from a long journey. What were your feelings? How did you spend your time waiting?

SITUATION

The final scenes in John's vision are of a crystal-clear river that flows from the throne of God into the New Jerusalem. The tree of life grows on its banks, and we see that what had once been forbidden to humankind in the Garden of Eden is now available for all to receive. The curse has forever been removed and all of God's people can now stand in his holy presence (see Revelation 22:1–3). John's amazing document has been called the "Revelation of Jesus Christ," primarily because that is the opening line in the book. However, because the word *of* in the title means "from" more than "about," we can think of its contents, particularly the last words, as a collection of "things Jesus revealed that he wants us to know." Had this book been named for the main theme we find in its pages, it could have been called the "Return of Jesus Christ."

OBSERVATION

Read Revelation 22:12–17 from the New International Version or the New King James Version.

NEW INTERNATIONAL VERSION

[12] "Look, I am coming soon! My reward is with me, and I will give to each person according to what they have done. [13] I am the Alpha and the Omega, the First and the Last, the Beginning and the End.

[14] "Blessed are those who wash their robes, that they may have the right to the tree of life and may go through the gates into the city. [15] Outside are the dogs, those who practice magic arts, the sexually immoral, the murderers, the idolaters and everyone who loves and practices falsehood.

[16] "I, Jesus, have sent my angel to give you this testimony for the churches. I am the Root and the Offspring of David, and the bright Morning Star."

[17] The Spirit and the bride say, "Come!" And let the one who hears say, "Come!" Let the one who is thirsty come; and let the one who wishes take the free gift of the water of life.

NEW KING JAMES VERSION

[12] "And behold, I am coming quickly, and My reward is with Me, to give to every one according to his work. [13] I am the Alpha and the Omega, the Beginning and the End, the First and the Last."

[14] Blessed are those who do His commandments, that they may have the right to the tree of life, and may enter through the gates into the city. [15] But outside are dogs and sorcerers and sexually immoral and murderers and idolaters, and whoever loves and practices a lie.

¹⁶ "I, Jesus, have sent My angel to testify to you these things in the churches. I am the Root and the Offspring of David, the Bright and Morning Star."

¹⁷ And the Spirit and the bride say, "Come!" And let him who hears say, "Come!" And let him who thirsts come. Whoever desires, let him take the water of life freely.

EXPLORATION

1. For what reason does Jesus say that he is coming back?

_____

_____

_____

_____

_____

2. Note all the names of Jesus given in this passage. What do these names for Jesus—Alpha and Omega, Offspring of David, Morning Star—reveal about him?

_____

_____

_____

_____

3. Read Matthew 25:14–30. What does it mean that Jesus will reward each person "according to what they have done" (Revelation 22:12)?

_____

_____

_____

_____

4. What does Jesus mean when he says, "Blessed are those who wash their robes, that they may have the right to the tree of life and may go through the gates" (verse 14)?

5. What kinds of people does Jesus say will be excluded from entering the New Jerusalem?

6. What are the benefits of eating from the tree of life and drinking the water of life?

INSPIRATION

Invitations are special. Some are casual, such as asking for a date. Some are significant, such as offering someone a job. Others are permanent, such as proposing marriage. But all are special.

Invitations. Words embossed on a letter: "You are invited to a gala celebrating the grand opening of . . ." Requests received in the mail: "Mr. and Mrs. John Smith request your presence at the wedding of their daughter . . ." Surprises over the phone: "Hey, Joe. I've got an extra ticket to the game. Interested?"

To receive an invitation is to be honored—to be held in high esteem. For that reason all invitations deserve a kind and thoughtful response.

But the most incredible invitations are not found in envelopes or fortune cookies, they are found in the Bible. You can't read about God without finding him issuing invitations. He invited Eve to marry Adam, the animals to enter the Ark, David to be king, Israel to leave bondage, Nehemiah to rebuild Jerusalem. God is an inviting God. He invited Mary to birth his son, the disciples to fish for men, the adulterous woman to start over, and Thomas to touch his wounds. God is the King who prepares the palace, sets the table, and invites his subjects to come in.

In fact, it seems his favorite word is *come*.

"*Come* now, and let us reason together . . . though your sins are like scarlet, they shall be as white as snow" (Isaiah 1:18 NKJV).

"Everyone who thirsts, *come* to the waters" (Isaiah 55:1 NKJV).

"*Come* to me, all you who are weary and burdened" (Matthew 11:28).

"*Come* to the wedding banquet" (Matthew 22:4).

"*Come* follow me . . . and I will send you out to fish for people" (Matthew 4:19).

"Let anyone who is thirsty *come* to me and drink" (John 7:37).

God is a God who invites. God is a God who calls. God is a God who opens the door and waves his hand pointing pilgrims to a full table.

His invitation is not just for a meal, however; it is for life. An invitation to come into his kingdom and take up residence in a tearless, graveless, painless world.

Who can come? Whoever wishes. The invitation is at once universal and personal. (From *And the Angels Were Silent* by Max Lucado.)

REACTION

7. What invitation does Jesus give to *all* people in this final passage from Revelation?

8. What does Jesus' invitation portray about God's salvation?

9. Even though Jesus states that he is coming quickly, why do you think he has delayed his return for more than 2,000 years (see 2 Peter 3:8–9)?

10. In what ways does your life demonstrate that you believe Jesus is returning?

11. What reward would you like to receive when Jesus returns?

12. What do you need to change in order to be prepared for Christ's return?

LIFE LESSONS

Jesus once told a parable about a homeowner whose house was burglarized. Jesus made the point that if the owner had *known* the thief was coming, he would have kept better watch and protected his valuables. Jesus' point was that we must keep constant watch, for we do not know the day or hour that he will return—but we can be sure that he *is* coming back. The best way to wait until that time is to be watchful, keep busy learning Jesus' commands and living them our every day, and join the prayers of others who say, "Come, Lord Jesus." We must live in continual expectation and anticipation of his return—and our own final homecoming.

DEVOTION

Father, we are anticipating your return with much excitement. Help us to keep busy doing the work that you have called us to do until that time and remain faithful to you while we wait. Come quickly, Lord, for we look forward to spending eternity with you!

JOURNALING

What are some things you will keep busy doing for God until Jesus returns to this earth?

_____

_____

_____

_____

_____

_____

_____

_____

_____

_____

_____

_____

_____

_____

_____

_____

_____

_____

_____

_____

_____

FOR FURTHER READING

To complete the book of Revelation during this twelve-part study, read Revelation 22:1–21. For more Bible passages on Christ's return, read Daniel 7:13–14; Zechariah 2:10– 11; Matthew 24:36–44; Luke 21:25–28; 1 Corinthians 15:50–57; 1 Thessalonians 4:13–18; Titus 2:11–14; Hebrews 9:97–28; and 1 Peter 1:6–7.

LEADER'S GUIDE FOR SMALL GROUPS

Thank you for your willingness to lead a group through *Life Lessons from Revelation*. The rewards of being a leader are different from those of participating, and we hope you find your own walk with Jesus deepened by this experience. During the twelve lessons in this study, you will guide your group through selected passages in Revelation and explore the key themes of the book. There are several elements in this leader's guide that will help you as you structure your study and reflection time, so be sure to follow along and take advantage of each one.

BEFORE YOU BEGIN

Before your first meeting, make sure the group members have their own copy of the *Life Lessons from Revelation* study guide so they can follow along and have their answers written out ahead of time. Alternately, you can hand out the guides at your first meeting and give the group some time to look over the material and ask any preliminary questions. Be sure to send a sheet around the room during that first meeting and have the members write down their name, phone number, and email address so you can keep in touch with them during the week.

There are several ways to structure the duration of the study. You can choose to cover each lesson individually for a total of twelve weeks of discussion, or you can combine two lessons together per week for a total of six weeks of discussion. You can also choose to have the group members read just the selected passages of Scripture given in each lesson, or they can cover the entire book of Revelation by reading the material listed in the "For Further Reading" section at the end of each lesson. The following table illustrates these options:

Twelve-Week Format

Week	Lessons Covered	Simplified Reading	Expanded Reading
1	A Vision of Christ	Revelation 1:9–20	Revelation 1:1–20
2	Your First Love	Revelation 2:1–7	Revelation 2:1–7
3	No Compromise	Revelation 2:8–17	Revelation 2:8–17
4	Standing for the Truth	Revelation 2:18–29	Revelation 2:18–29
5	Persevering for Christ	Revelation 3:1–13	Revelation 3:1–13
6	Vibrant Faith	Revelation 3:14–22	Revelation 3:14–4:11
7	Worshiping God	Revelation 5:8–14	Revelation 5:1–9:21
8	Patient Endurance	Revelation 14:1–13	Revelation 10:1–14:13
9	The Defeat of Evil	Revelation 19:11–21	Revelation 14:14–19:21
10	All Things Made New	Revelation 21:1–8	Revelation 20:1–21:8
11	An Eternal Dwelling	Revelation 21:9–27	Revelation 21:9–27
12	Jesus Is Returning	Revelation 22:12–17	Revelation 22:1–21

Six-Week Format

Week	Lessons Covered	Simplified Reading	Expanded Reading
1	A Vision of Christ / Your First Love	Revelation 1:9–2:7	Revelation 1:1–2:7
2	No Compromise / Standing for the Truth	Revelation 2:8–29	Revelation 2:8–29
3	Persevering for Christ / Vibrant Faith	Revelation 3:1–22	Revelation 3:1–4:11
4	Worshiping God / Patient Endurance	Revelation 5:8–14; 14:1–13	Revelation 5:1–14:13
5	The Defeat of Evil / All Things Made New	Revelation 19:11–21; 21:1–8	Revelation 14:14–21:8
6	An Eternal Dwelling / Jesus Is Returning	Revelation 21:9–22:17	Revelation 21:9–22:21

Generally, the ideal size you will want for the group is between eight to ten people, which ensures everyone will have enough time to participate in discussions. If you have more people, you might want to break up the main group into smaller subgroups. Encourage those who show up at the first meeting to commit to attending the duration of the study, as this will help the group members get to know each other, create stability for the group, and help you know how to prepare each week.

Each of the lessons begins with a brief reflection that highlights the theme you will be discussing that week. As you begin your group time, have the group members briefly respond to the opening question to get them thinking about the topic at hand. Some people may want to tell a long story in response to one of these questions, but the goal is to keep the answers brief. Ideally, you want everyone in the group to get a chance to answer, so try to keep the responses to just a few minutes. If you have more talkative group members, say up front that everyone needs to limit his or her answer to two minutes.

Give the group members a chance to answer, but tell them to feel free to pass if they wish. With the rest of the study, it's generally not a good idea to have everyone answer every question—a free-flowing discussion is more desirable. But with the opening reflection question, you can go around the circle. Encourage shy people to share, but don't force them.

Before your first meeting, let the group members know how the lessons are broken down. During your group discussion time the members will be drawing on the answers they wrote to the Exploration and Reaction sections, so encourage them to always complete these ahead of time. Also, invite them to bring any questions and insights they uncovered while reading to your next meeting, especially if they had a breakthrough moment or if they didn't understand something they read.

WEEKLY PREPARATION

As the leader, there are a few things you should do to prepare for each meeting:

- *Read through the lesson.* This will help you to become familiar with the content and know how to structure the discussion times.
- *Decide which questions you want to discuss.* Depending on how you structure your group time, you may not be able to cover every question. So select the questions ahead of time that you absolutely want the group to explore.
- *Be familiar with the questions you want to discuss.* When the group meets you'll be watching the clock, so you want to make sure you are familiar with the Bible study questions you have selected. You can then spend time in the passage again when the group meets. In this way, you'll ensure you have the passage more deeply in your mind than your group members.
- *Pray for your group.* Pray for your group members throughout the week and ask God to lead them as they study his Word.
- *Bring extra supplies to your meeting.* The members should bring their own pens for writing notes, but it's a good idea to have extras available for those who forget. You may also want to bring paper and additional Bibles.

Note that in many cases there will not be one "right" answer to the question. Answers will vary, especially when the group members are being asked to share their personal experiences.

STRUCTURING THE DISCUSSION TIME

You will need to determine with your group how long you want to meet each week so you can plan your time accordingly. Generally, most groups like to meet for either sixty minutes or ninety minutes, so you could use one of the following schedules:

Section	60 Minutes	90 Minutes
WELCOME (members arrive and get settled)	5 minutes	10 minutes
REFLECTION (discuss the opening question for the lesson)	10 minutes	15 minutes
DISCUSSION (discuss the Bible study questions in the Exploration and Reaction sections)	35 minutes	50 minutes
PRAYER/CLOSING (pray together as a group and dismiss)	10 minutes	15 minutes

As the group leader, it is up to you to keep track of the time and keep things moving along according to your schedule. You might want to set a timer for each segment so both you and the group members know when your time is up. (Note that there are some good phone apps for timers that play a gentle chime or other pleasant sound instead of a disruptive noise.) Don't feel pressured to cover every question you have selected if the group has a good discussion going. Again, it's not necessary to go around the circle and make everyone share.

Don't be concerned if the group members are silent or slow to share. People are often quiet when they are pulling together their ideas, and this might be a new experience for them. Just ask a question and let it hang in the air until someone shares. You can then say, "Thank you. What about others? What came to you when you reflected on the passage?"

GROUP DYNAMICS

Leading a group through *Life Lessons from Revelation* will prove to be highly rewarding both to you and your group members—but that doesn't mean you will not encounter any challenges along the way! Discussions can get off track. Group members may not be sensitive to the needs and ideas of others. Some might worry they will be expected to talk about matters that make them feel awkward. Others may express comments that result in disagreements. To help ease this strain on you and the group, consider the following ground rules:

- When someone raises a question or comment that is off the main topic, suggest you deal with it another time, or, if you feel led to go in that direction, let the group know you will be spending some time discussing it.
- If someone asks a question you don't know how to answer, admit it and move on. At your discretion, feel free to invite group members to comment on questions that call for personal experience.
- If you find one or two people are dominating the discussion time, direct a few questions to others in the group. Outside the main group time, ask the more dominating members to help you draw out the quieter ones. Work to make them a part of the solution instead of the problem.
- When a disagreement occurs, encourage the group members to process the matter in love. Encourage those on opposite sides to restate what they heard the other side say about the matter, and then invite each side to evaluate if that perception is accurate. Lead the group in examining other Scriptures related to the topic and look for common ground.

When any of these issues arise, encourage your group members to follow the words from the Bible: "Love one another" (John 13:34), "If it is possible, as far as it depends on you, live at peace with everyone" (Romans 12:18), and, "Be quick to listen, slow to speak and slow to become angry" (James 1:19).

Thank you again for taking the time to lead your group. May God reward your efforts and dedication and make your time together in this study fruitful for his kingdom.

Also Available in the Life Lessons Series

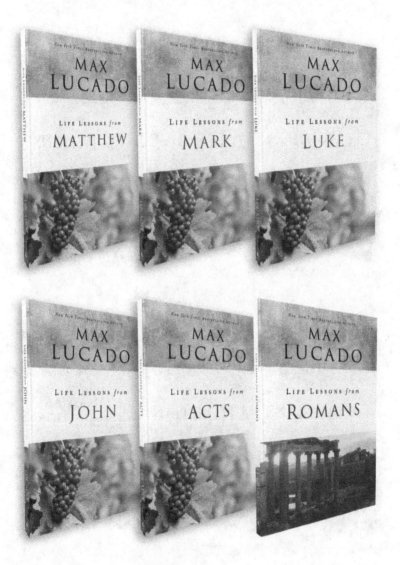

Now available wherever books and ebooks are sold.

ALSO AVAILABLE IN THE
LIFE LESSONS SERIES

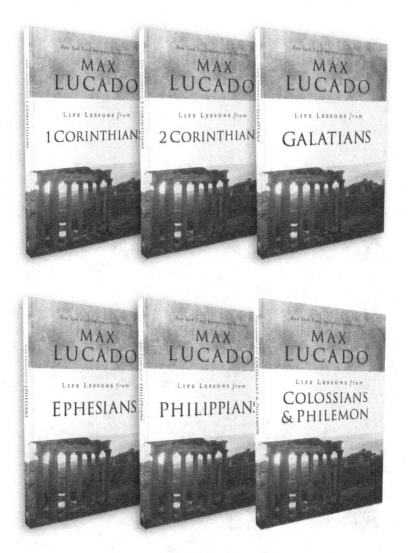

*Now available wherever books
and ebooks are sold.*